COMPLETE
Tang Soo Do
MANUAL From White Belt to Black Belt - Vol. 1

with "The Great Warrior"
Grand Master HO SIK PAK
Hwa Rang World Tang Soo Do Moo Duk Kwan Federation

with "The Great Warrior"
Grand Master HO SIK PAK

**Complete Tang Soo Do Manual -
From White Belt to Black Belt
with "The Great Warrior"
Grand Master HO SIK PAK, Volume 1**

by **Grand Master Ho Sik Pak**

Published by
High Mountain Publishing
California, USA

Printed in the USA

**International Standard Book Number
Hardcover Edition**
0-9718609-0-4
Paperback Edition
0-9718609-6-3

First Printing
September 2002
Second Printing
May 2004
Third Printing
March 2011

Writers
John Dorsey
Lukas Martisius
Ursula Escher

Photography
Ho Sik Pak
Ursula Escher

**Book Layout & Design
and Cover Design**
Ursula Escher

Models for Photography
Bryan Mc Daniels
Cowen Bailey
Evan Henzi
Ho Sik Pak
Keiko Kang
Kyle Pak
Michael Mendoza
Ray Laureano
Robn Meeks
Ursula Escher

Tang
Soo
Do
Moo
Duk
Kwan

This is the book that you have been waiting for. It will guide you from basic stances to black belt combination techniques

이 한권의 책이 자신과 남의 생명을 건지는데, 그리고 건강한 삶을 영위하는데 사용된다면 이책의 저자로써 사명을 다했음을 자부하겠습니다.

Best wishes

박 홍 석

Contents

1. Acknowledgements

One night I was driving two children and myself to an acting class in Burbank, California. As I was driving, I saw a young man and woman holding a baby, standing in the middle of the street. I watched as a group of six men surrounded the couple. One of the men hit the young man in the jaw and he fell to the ground. He tried to get up, and was hit again. The woman tried to help her husband, still holding the baby in her arms, and another man raised his hand to hit her. My concern for the baby brought me out of the car, immediately assuming fighting position. As the thought of the baby falling to the ground flew through my mind, I let out a *Ki hap* so loud that I caught the attention of the entire scene. I walked over to the men, furious with the idea that they could harm an innocent family, and asked, "What are you doing?" I told the family to go home, and they abruptly left me with the six men. I expected them to attack me, but to my surprise, they stood staring as I began to lecture them (watching their every move, of course). My lecture concluded and I got back into my car and drove away. It was a lucky situation for all who were involved. The couple and their baby were lucky because they walked away alive, those six guys were lucky because I did not have to beat them up, and I was lucky because I was not stabbed or shot.

Tang Soo Do has given me the chance to save people's lives on other occasions, and the courage and confidence to know that I need to share my knowledge with future generations.

Christmas Group Photo, 2001.

I would like to acknowledge the following people who made this book happen: I would like to thank the founder of Tang Soo Do, Grand Master Hwang Kee, my master, Grand Master Lee Pal Yong, and my seniors, juniors, and students. Special thanks to Ursula Escher, Lukas Martisius, John Dorsey, and all the students that put time into this book.

Thank you very much for sharing your knowledge and helping me make this possible.

Good luck, best wishes and God bless.
Sincerely,

Grand Master Ho Sik Pak

2. Foreword

Grand Master Pak in 'Pyung Ahn' (piece of mind), New Zealand, Dec 2003

By
Rockne S. O'Bannon
March 1, 2002

At the time of this writing, my son Eric and I have been students under Grand Master Ho Sik Pak for just about a year. Eric, nine years old presently, started with Tang Soo Do to strengthen his legs and to help with his coordination. I had been looking for some sort of regular conditioning exercise program that, ideally, was also challenging. And fun. So, having observed one of my son's classes and witnessing Grand Master Pak's method of instruction, I joined up and began the semi-weekly classes beside my son. And today, I'm proud to say, we've both attained 5th Gup (green belts with one stripe).

I'm a film screenwriter and director, creator of the television series 'Farscape', 'SeaQuest DSV', and 'Alien Nation'. Much of my day is spent sitting at a desk, or sitting in meetings, or sitting on the set waiting for the next scene to be shot. In other words, I sit. A lot. My twice weekly training sessions are a welcome chance to work out the kinks, get my heart racing, and train toward the goal of black belt.

Grand Master Pak is a remarkable teacher. No other word for it. Remarkable. I marvel at his skill teaching students at a very wide range of ages. He's exacting yet patient; firm yet compassionate; challenging yet encouraging. To attain the levels of mastery in the very rigorous martial art of Tang Soo Do as Grand Master Pak has, is in itself, quite an accomplishment. But to also be able to teach others as expertly as he does, is, well, remarkable. There's that word again. Through his teaching and our studies this past year, Eric and I have increased our physical strength, our endurance, our concentration, and our sense of personal discipline.

Our Federation is founded on Ten Key Concepts:

1. Courage
2. Endurance
3. Concentration
4. Honesty
5. Humility
6. Control of Power
7. Tension and Relaxation
8. Speed Control
9. Justice
10. Best Friendship

A man could lead a true quality life following these concepts.

The book you hold in your hand is the result of Grand Master Pak's passion, his dedication, his love of the art and discipline of Tang Soo Do. My son and I could have no better teacher. And now, by way of this book, you have him as your teacher, too.

By
Robin Dunne
March 28, 2002

I am a film and television actor ('Dawson's Creek', 'Mark Twain's Roughing It', 'The Big Hit') and have been a member of Hwa Rang World Tang Soo Do Moo Duk Kwan Federation for eight months now. I have had an interest in pursuing Martial Arts for many years and have studied intermittently, but I never found a school, or style that was right for me until now. I found other schools much too strict, impersonal, and not particularly good environments for learning. In the short time since joining Grand Master Ho Sik Pak's federation I feel that I've gotten a strong foothold in learning Tang Soo Do, and I feel that I am on my way to becoming a "Great Warrior".

What I like about Grand Master Pak's school is that, while he instills in us the rules and respect of learning the martial art, it also is a friendly environment where we don't forget to have fun. The members of Grand Master Pak's school have formed a bond that is almost like a family, where everyone is encouraged to help each other move forward. In many ways the federation functions as one unit.

Another aspect of Grand Master Pak's teaching that helps students form a greater understanding of Tang Soo Do, is the emphasis on not only the physical movements (forms, kicks, etc.) but also on the philosophy of Tang Soo Do. In studying the philosophy of Tang Soo Do (like the "Key Concepts" etc.) students acquire a more rounded understanding of what they are doing. Mind, body and spirit working together.

Learning a Martial Art is something that truly changes your life, and not only makes you physically flexible and strong, but also strengthens your mind. I would encourage anyone interested in learning Martial Arts to join Hwa Rang Moo Duk Kwan Federation, as Grand Master Pak is one of the most dedicated teachers I have had the privilege of learning from.

Grand Master Pak and Robin Dunne.

Rockne and his son Erick O'Bannon

③ Biography of Grand Master Pak

Grand Master Ho Sik Pak began his study of Tang Soo Do Moo Duk Kwan at the age of 10 in Yong Mun, a small town in Kyung Ki province of South Korea. He was awarded Cho Dan at the age of 13 and continued his study there until 1977.

From 1977 to 1979, Grand Master Pak served in the Korean Army and taught combat and self-defense skills to his fellow servicemen. Following his discharge from the military, he was employed as an instructor of Tang Soo Do at the American Air Force Base in Kun San province, Jun Ra Buk Do, South Korea. There he taught those same techniques to U.S. Military Personnel until 1982.

In 1982, he was chosen as a member of the Korean Olympic Tang Soo Do team and traveled to the International Tang Soo Do Championship in Atlantic City, New Jersey, contributing to the team's victory. At this time, he decided to make the United States his permanent residence and moved to Southern California.

Since 1982, he has been the owner and Master Instructor of several separate studios, including his first in Woodland Hills, California and his current location in Canoga Park, California. He trained in Korean Soo Bahk Do Association beginning in 1966. He belonged to the U.S. Tang Soo Do Moo Duk Kwan Federation, now called the U.S. Soo Bahk Do Federation, from 1982 to 1994. He founded the Hwa Rang World Tang Soo Do Moo Duk Kwan Federation in 1994, and he continues as its President and Master Examiner today. Since the Federation's formation, the following studios have joined as affiliates: Master Dixson in Sacramento, California; Master Jack Pistella, Master Ed Samane, Master Eric and Master Robert Kovaleski in Pennsylvania; Kyosa Vince Don Vito in California; Kyosa Anthony Sagun in Oahu, Hawaii; Master Francis in Aruba, Caribbean; and Master Alfried Paulina in Curacao, Caribbean. The Hwa Rang World Tang Soo Do Federation is growing worldwide as one of the most efficient and strongest foundations for traditional Korean martial arts.

Ho Sik Pak at the age of 15.

In addition to Grand Master Pak's teaching responsibilities, he has been featured in many martial arts motion pictures, such as 'Best of the Best'. Most recently, he starred in the featured-length film, 'Hunt to Kill'.

In 1997 and 1999 he released a full line of **Instructional Videos** (page 234) in traditional Tang Soo Do and other training techniques. In 2002 he published the **Complete Tang Soo Do Manual, Volume 1**. And in 2003 he produced the book **Self-Defense for Kids**.

In 2003 he become officially listed in the *Kington's National Register of Who's Who* for his expertise, his outstanding achievements nationally and in the community.

On July 19th 2003 Grand Master Pak celebrated his 8th Dan at Battle of LA, National Martial Arts Championship, in Woodland Hills, CA. This annual event is hosted and promoted by GM Pak.

Grand Master Ho Sik Pak at the age of 17 after winning National Grand Championship

Grand Master Pak, 18, doing a flying side kick through a fire ring and obstacles.

Performing Snake Form

Grand Master Pak's Photo Album

1976, Grand Master Pak (2nd person from bottom right) as his school's commander.

With nephew, Young Hwan Pak, at his Elementary Graduation.

As a Commander in a Street Parade - Yong Mun High School was the winning School.

Celebration before Grand Master Lee Pal Yong departure to Malaysia as a special instructor.

Gup Testing - Grand Master Lee (1st), Grand Master Pak (3rd) and Grand Master Hwang Kee (4th) and Grand Master Kim (8th). 1981 - at the Kun San Air Force Base, South Korea.

After testing at the Kun San Air Force Base with Grand Master Lee Hon In and Master Choi.

Grand Master Pak, 22, demonstrating speed breaking. The wooden stick was placed on the top of a cup and an egg on each side.

Gup and Dan Testing at the Kun San Air Force Base, 1981.

After demonstration in Santa Barbara, CA.

Grand Master Pak performing an obstacle jump side kick.

Standing on eggs and breaking board with sword.

Performing with nephew Young Hwan Pak *Rohai* Form.

Round House kick to cigarette and Spinning Back Hook Kick to can.

'United Airlines' commercial - Holding Korean Flag.

United Airlines commercial

Scene from 'Big Trouble in Little China'.

Scene from 'Hunt to Kill'.

Set from 'Hunt to Kill'.

Demonstrating Acupuncture.

NATIONAL/INTERNATIONAL
TANG SOO DO CHAMPIONSHIPS
NOVEMBER 20-21, 1982
ATLANTIC CITY, NEW JERSEY, U.S.A.

1982
U.S. TANG SOO DO MOO DUK KWAN
FEDERATION, INC.

**Book Cover of Tang Soo Do Olympics -
Atlantic City, NJ**

KOREA

Sa Bom Kun Ho Yoo
Official

Sa Bom Hyuk Yoon Kwon
Official

Yong Jin Kim

Ho Bok Pak

Hee Yong Lee

Dae Kyu Jang

**Member of Korean
Olympic Team.**

One inch breaking with a jump hook kick, then another breaking on the ground. 1982 International Tournament, Atlantic City, NJ.

Hee Il Cho Beverly Hills Open Tournament -
Demonstration with Simon Rhee.

Demonstration with Peking Wu Shu Demo Team.

**Competing *Ssi Rum* (Korean
Wrestling). Winning moment
of Grand Champion.**

Championship at West Point with cadets.

Breaking Form Demo.

Grand Master Lee Pal Yong, Grand Master Pak's Master.

Legends of Tang Soo Do Grand Masters.

Testing Committee - Region 9 (California), US Tang Soo Do Moo Duk Kwan Federation.

Shooting commercial with John Ratzenberger.

X-Mas Banquet Demo at Pak's Karate Studio.

Choreographing scene for In Pyo Cha,
(#1 korean actor). Year 2002.

10th Dan Testing.
Hwa Rang World Tang Soo Do
Moo Duk Kwan Federation
Year 2000.

After Seminar with Master Elfried Paulina (left) and Master Francis Frans (right). Aruba,Caribbean.

Seminar in Sacramento, CA with Master Dixson.

Seminars in Pennsylvania, USA.

Gup Testing, Pak's Karate Studio, 2003.

Seminar in Scranton, PA.

Master Jack Pistella, Pennsylvania, USA.

Gang from Pak's Karate Studio, 2003.

4. Credits & Awards

● TV and Film

Motion Pictures
VIOLATED - Violated Production - Jury Member
KILL ZONE - Spartan Films - Supporting Soldier
3:15 - Raleigh Studios - Supporting & High School Gang Leader
REVENGE OF THE STOLEN STAR - Six Stars Productions - Co-Star - Prince
NIGHT STALKER - Night Stalker Productions - Martial Arts Fighter
MAXIE - Marions Wall Productions - Martial Arts Fighter
BIG TROUBLE IN LITTLE CHINA - 20th Century Fox - Fighter
HOLLYWOOD COP - Peacock Film Productions - Chinese Mafia Leader
SPIES - Lorimar Tele-Pictures - Stunt Fighter
NOBLE HOUSE - Deg - Principal
LOOK AT ME AMERICA - Richard Parks Production - Co-Star
BEST OF THE BEST - Taurus Entertainment Company - Co-Star
MORTAL KOMBAT - Katja Motion Picture Corp. - Warrior
IRON PALM- Stunt double - Choreographer - Magic Lantern Productions

Television
THE MASTER - Viacom Productions - Bodyguard-Waiter-Terrorist
THE LONG TIME GONE - Viacom Productions - Lover
ME AND MOM - Viacom Productions - Tourist
UNDER SUSPICION - ABC Circle Star Film - Businessman
MR. SUCCESS - Viacom Productions - Businessman
HAPPY BIRTHDAY RAY - Karson-Higgings-Shaw Co. - College Student

From the movie
'Best of the Best' (1989).

Industrial
U.S. MILITARY SERVICE - Goal Productions - Lead Soldier
MARTIAL ARTS EDUCATION FILM - Wolfe Productions - Lead

Commercials
MILLER LITE BEER - Bob Giraldi Productions - Spectator
UNITED AIRLINES - Robert Abel Associates - Flag Dancer

Tang Soo Do 20-Video Series by GM Pak.

LA CHOY SOY SAUCE - Vern Gillum Productions - Martial Arts Fighter
COORS EXTRA GOLD - Michael Daniel Productions - Brick Breaker
NESCAFE - Martial Arts Instructor
MIND ARROW CO - Martial Arts Fighter

Awards & Credits
"BEST INSTRUCTOR AND PERFORMER IN MARTIAL ARTS"
MASTER EXPO U.S. KARATE INVITATIONAL DEMONSTRATION - PRINCIPAL, DIRECTOR, PRODUCER, AND CHOREOGRAPHER

Special Abilities
Pro-Ping-Pong, Volleyball, Soccer, Golf, Ice Skating, Roller Skating, Handball, Basketball, Bicycle Riding, Horseback Riding, Stunt Fighting, Dancing, Gymnastics

● Teaching Experience

2002 - 2003	Seminars in Pennsylvania, Arizona, California, Oregon and Korea
1994	Grand Master and Founder **HWA RANG WORLD TANG SOO DO MOO DUK KWAN FEDERATION**, Canoga Park, CA
1999 - 2002	Seminars in Sacramento, Arizona, Pennsylvania, etc…
1989 - 2002	Pak's Karate Studio
1989 - 1994	Instructor for Private Studios, CA
1985 - 1989	Martial Arts Instructor, Woodland Hills, CA
1984 - 1985	Instructor for Private Studios, CA
Sept - 1985	Little Tokyo, LA - Invitational Demonstration
June - 1985	Demonstration - 2nd Southern California Championship
1982 - 1984	Instructor for American Air Forces Base, in the U.S.
1980 - 1982	Instructor for American Air Force Base, in Republic of Korea
1977 - 1980	Instructor for Korean Special Forces
1975 - 1977	Instructor for Yong Mun Studio in Kyong Ki Providence

Dan and Kodanja (Master) Testing July 2000

Credentials

July - 2003	8th Dan Promotion at Battle of LA, National Championship

July - 2003   8th Dan Promotion at Battle of LA, National Championship
Jan - 2003   GM Pak officially listed in the *Kingston's National Register of Who's Who*
Dec - 2000   Most Awarded Studio in World Open Martial Arts Championship
Mar - 1999   Grand Champion - LA Open
July - 1998   Grand Champion - Pacific Coast Grand National, California
July - 1995   1st Place Master Division - Ed Parkers International, California
Dec - 1995   1st Place - Gabe Reynaga's Karate Championship
July - 1988   1st Place - Ed Parkers International Championship
July - 1987   Grand Champion - Ed Parkers International, California
July - 1986   1st Place Ed Parkers International, California
July - 1985   1st Place Ed Parkers International, California
Aug - 1985   Grand Champion - West Coast Invitational, California
Aug - 1985   Japanese Town in San Francisco Invitational Demonstration
July - 1985   Top Ranking Competitor - Ed Parker's Invitational Long Beach Karate Tournament
June - 1985   1st Place and Best Form Performance - LA Open
Dec - 1984   2-1st Places - Simon Rhee's Open Tournament
Nov - 1984   1st Place - Imperial Dragon Martial Art Open Tournament
Oct - 1984   Grand Champion - Vo Lam Kung Fu Open Championship
Sept - 1984   Grand Champion - American Traditional Martial Way Champion
Aug - 1984   1st Place - Southern California Summer Karate Champion
June - 1984   Championship Award - Ed Parker's International Long Beach Karate Tournament
June - 1984   Selected along with Simon Rhee as a member of the Korean Demonstration Team performing with the "The World Famous Peking Wu Shu Team"
June - 1984   Grand Champion - Simom Rhee's Open Tournament
May - 1984   Grand Champion - Hard Style Form Competition in Master Cho's Beverly Hills, CA Open Tournament
April - 1984   World Famous MASTER EXPO California Invitation Demonstration
Nov - 1983   Officiated at U.S. TANG SOO DO Tournament in San Diego, California Special Demonstration
Dec - 1982   1st Place - Member of the KOREAN TEAM
               Officiated at WORLD TOURNAMENT in Atlantic City, NJ
June - 1982   1st Place - KOREAN NATIONAL TOURNAMENT
July - 1981   1st Place - Free Style Form - Seoul City, Korea
Jan - 1981   BODY BUILDING CHAMPION AS MR KUN SAN (see page 233)
Sept - 1980   1st Place - Individual Free Sparring Form and National Team
Sept - 1979   1st Place - Korean Special Forces Championship
Oct - 1978   1st Place - Korean National Championship
Sept - 1976   Grand Champion - Korean National Tournament
Sept - 1975   1st Place - Individual Free Sparring, Free Form and Team
Sept - 1973   Grand Champion - Form and Free Sparring - Nationals, Seoul, Korea

Special Abilities

Weapons: Samurai Sword, Nunchuku, Long Stick, Short Stick, Tonfa, Yaskumira, Sai, Throwing Star, Tonfa, Rope Techniques.
Techniques: Tang Soo Do, Tae Kwon Do, Hap ki Do, Yu Do, Korean Wrestling.

Grand Master Chuck Norris, Grand Master Ho Sik Pak, and Grand Master Hee Il Cho.

From the movie "Best of the Best" (1989) Korean Marines with Korean Olympic Team.

Grand Master Tada Shi Yamashita, Grand Master Ho Sik Pak, and Grand Master Steven Seagal.

5. Korean, American and Federation Flags

The training uniform is traditionally adorned with two flags. The Korean flag, sewn on the upper left sleeve, symbolizes the country where Tang Soo Do originated. The student's national flag is fixed to the right upper sleeve. For our organization, this flag mainly is the American flag since most of the Federation's affiliate studios are American. Below are the meanings of the two flags.

The flag of the Republic of Korea - the *Taegukki*

The South Korean flag is probably one of the most philosophical in the world. The white background represents Confucian purity and peace, or the Buddist concept of "emptiness". The concept of "emptiness" is an important one in martial arts since one must empty one's mind of preconceived notions before martial arts training, then teachings can truly be learned. In the center of the flag lies a *Taeguk*, the Taoist symbol for balance and harmony. The symbols in the corners, known as *kwae*, were borrowed from the ancient book of Chinese thought, the "Classic of Changes" (Korean: the *Chu Yok*; Chinese: the *I Ching*). As with the central *Uhm/Yang* symbol, the four *kwae* also represent harmony and balance as shown below.

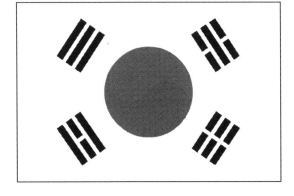

Kun representing Heaven - Creative.

Yi representing Fire-Loyal love, lying opposite to Water.

Kam representing Water - Treacherous Danger.

Kon represents Earth - Receptive, lying diagonally opposite to Heaven-Creative.

Red half represents **Yang** (heaven, day, male, heat, active, etc.) while the blue half is the opposite **Yin** (earth, night, female, cold, passive, etc.). The *Yin* and the *Yang* both circle one another in perfect balanced harmony.

The flag of the United States of America

The American flag symbolizes the gaining of independence, national unity, and the principals of justice, purity, and courage. The Continental Congress established the first flag in 1777. Although the American flag has undergone changes, the basic design is a pattern of white stars on a blue shield, and 13 rows of horizontal stripes.

The blue field represents justice, preservation, and vigilance.

White stars represent states in the union; stars are ancient symbols for sovereignty.

Each stripe represents one of the 13 colonies that declared independence from Great Britain in 1776. The red symbolizes strength and courage, while white represents innocence.

Federation Flag -
Hwa Rang World Tang Soo Do Moo Duk Kwan

The Federation flag was created by Grand Master Pak in 1994.

Hwa Rang (Flower of Manhood): Our ancestors (great warriors) from Shilla Dynasty.

6 berries: 6 continents.

13 leaves: 13 korean original provinces.

Kicking person on globe: Our goal is to teach next generations to the whole world.

Moo(center): Martial Art / Military Art.

Tang Soo (sides): Our Art.
"The way of the Tang dynasty open Hand"
Tang: Tang Dynasty of China.
Soo: Open Hand, weaponless combat.

6. Tang Soo Do Timeline

Pre-AD Period	Ancient Korean martial arts develop, influenced by Chinese styles.
37-935 AD	Three Kingdom Eras. *Soo Bahk* practiced by *Hwa Rang* warriors of the Shilla Kingdom.
1392-1910	Yi Dynasty. Other forms of martial arts develop along with *Soo Bahk*, e.g. *Tae Kyun*, *Soo Byuck*.
1909-1945	Japanese occupation. Korean martial arts suppressed, undergound training begins as a result.
1945	Korean independence. Hwang Kee establishes *Tang Soo Do Moo Duk Kwan*. Other schools formed, e.g. *Gi Do Kwan*, *Song Moo Kwan*, *Jung Do Kwan*, *Chosun Yonmu Kwan*, *Kwonbopbu*, *Kaesong*.
Post 1950's	*Tang Soo do Moo Duk Kwan* spreads worldwide.
1961	Korean government attempts to unify all martial art schools in single organization - *Tae Soo Do*. Hwang Kee keeps *Tang Soo Do Moo Duk Kwan* separate.
1965	The name *Tae Soo Do* changed to *Tae Kwon Do*.
Post 1960's	Various *Tang Soo Do* organizations form worldwide.
1994	Ho Sik Pak establishes the **Hwa Rang World Tang Soo Do Moo Duk Kwan Federation**.

7. History of Korean Tang Soo Do

● History of Tang Soo Do Moo Duk Kwan

Like most of Korea's martial art styles, the origins of modern Tang Soo Do are rooted in ancient times, however its development is obscure. Most historians of Tang Soo Do agree that this art began around two thousand years ago with the ancient art of Soo Bahk, and heavily influenced by Chinese martial art styles. Hence the name Tang Soo Do meaning "The way of the Tang dynasty open hand".

During the first century BC, the Korean Peninsula was divided into three kingdoms. Koguryo (37 BC-668 AD) was the largest, located in the north, and included portions of modern day China. In the south were the two smaller Kingdoms of Paekche (18 BC-660 AD) and Shilla (57 BC-935 AD). The era of the Three Kingdoms lasted for four centuries during which Korean arts and culture flourished. Each kingdom also kept busy repelling invaders, so martial arts also developed, becoming an important part of the culture. Many murals and statues from this period depict warriors in poses that resemble many stances seen in modern Tang Soo Do.

During the 7th Century, Shilla joined forces with the Tang Dynasty of China to over throw Paekche and Koguryo. But the Chinese had other ambitions - to take over and control Shilla. This was not to be. The Shilla army was able to repel the Chinese, and went on to unify the entire peninsula.

The Hwa Rang warriors were a key component of the Shilla military system during this dynasty. The Hwa Rang, loosely translated as "flowering manhood" were a paramilitary organization of aristocratic youth devoted to serving their king and country. Members of this organization were selected through contests, and lived together studying arts, culture, and training in all forms of military combat including a weaponless fighting called *Soo* (Hand/Water) *Bahk* (Hard/Shell) - hand techniques. The Hwa Rang followed a five-part code of honor written by the monk Won Kwang approximately 1,800 years ago:

- *Nara Eh Chung Sung*....... Be loyal to ones country and community
- *Boo Moo Eh Hyo Do*....... Obey ones parents, elders and teachers
- *Boung Woo Yu Shin*......... Honor friendship, including brothers and sisters
- *Im Jun Moo Toi*.............. Do not retreat in battle
- *Sal Sang Yoo Taek*.......... In killing, choose with justice and honor

This code forms the philosophical basis of Tang Soo Do today as reflected in the Ten Articles of Faith (page 35) adopted by most Tang Soo Do organizations. Although these codes have been adopted to modern times, the meaning of these five codes remain, providing a clear path to follow. Here in also lays a set of ideals that contain the precepts of Tang Soo Do.

The unified Shilla kingdom eventually was overthrown by the warlord Wang Kun in 918 AD, thus establishing the Koryo Dynasty that lasted until 1392 AD. During this dynasty, martial arts flourished, becoming integrated into the military and social fabric of the times. Soo Bahk was practiced not only as a fighting component for the military, but as a skill to improve people's physical and mental health and as a competitive sports activity. As a demonstration of national support, the royal family often arranged public demonstrations of martial arts by military personnel and Soo Bahk masters.

Illustration of one of the many Kwon Bup (fist) and Kon Bang (long stick) fighting techniques illustrated in the Muye Dobo Tongji.

The Yi Dynasty became established in 1392 and lasted until the Japanese occupation of the peninsula in 1910. During this period, the study of martial arts declined as more emphasis was placed on literature, music, and the arts. Soo Bahk practice became decentralized, little support was given to the development of military science, and martial arts generally were looked down upon by the ruling class. The only official martial art practiced during this time was archery.

During the latter part of the Yi Dynasty, the country was invaded by the Japanese (1592-1598), followed by two Chinese invasions from Manchu in 1627 and 1636. Military science was revived, and by order of the ruling kings, a series of military manuals depicting military fighting skills were developed. The series culminated with the writing of the Muye Dobo Tongji (Comprehensive Illustrated Manual of Martial Arts) as ordered by King Jungjo and written by Yi Duk-moo and Park Je-ga in 1790.

The Mooye Dobo Tong Ji describes and illustrates 23 fighting systems incorporating various spears, swords and flails used on foot or from horseback, shields, long stick, and hand and foot techniques. The latter were referred to as Kwon Bup (Fist fighting Method). The authors of the Mooye Dobo Tong Ji described how the various Kwon Bup techniques were derived from older Soo Bahk fist fighting and Chinese techniques taught at the Shaolin Temple since the Tang and Song Dynasties.

The Yi Dynasty collapsed with the invasion of the Japanese in 1909. Korean arts and culture were suppressed by the Japanese, including Korean martial arts. The Koreans continued to practice Soo Bahk and other styles, but only underground.

The end of the Japanese occupation saw the birth of modern Tang Soo Do. During the occupation, a martial artist by the name of Hwang Kee studied Soo Bahk and Tae Kyun as a young man, then traveled to China where he studied Kung Fu under Master Yang, Kuk Jin. During these years, he was able to travel throughout Korea by working for the railroad, and was able to study some books on Okinawan Karate.

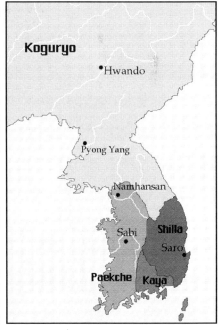

**KOREA
350 AD
"The Three Kingdoms"**

In 1945, Grand Master Hwang Kee formed the Tang Soo Do Moo Duk Kwan Federation. He formed the modern Tang Soo Do by incorporating fighting principals from Soo Bahk Do (as described in the Kwon Bup Chong Do), and techniques from northern and southern Chinese Kung Fu. He incorporated this martial art system and associated philosophy into his Moo Duk Kwan school of martial arts. The Chinese characters for Moo Duk Kwan translate into the "Institute of Martial Virtue". Since then, Grand Master Hwang Kee has spread the art of Tang Soo Do throughout the world where its philosophy is practiced on nearly every continent.

● Illustrations of Sword, Long Stick, Spear and Other Weapons. Also Kwon Bup (fist) techniques in the Mooye Dobo Tong Ji.

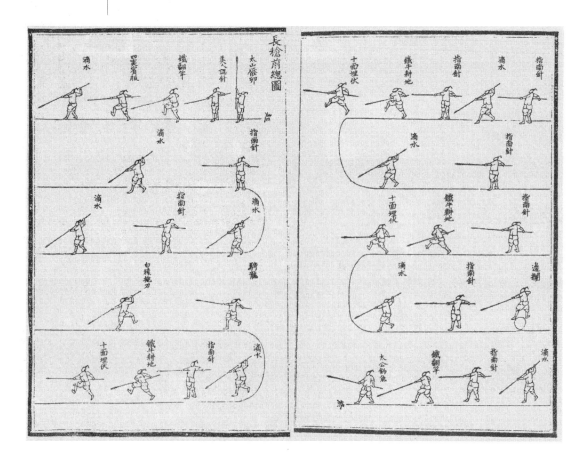

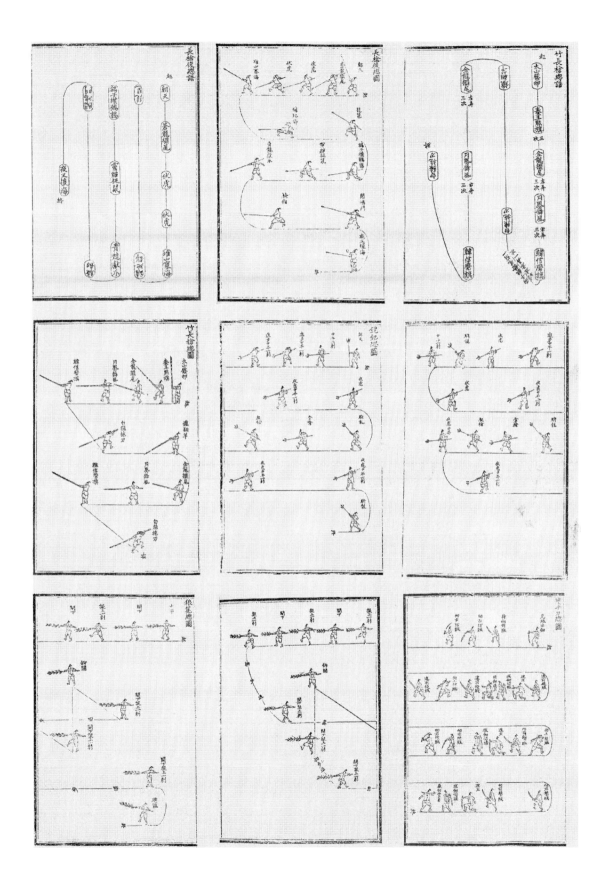

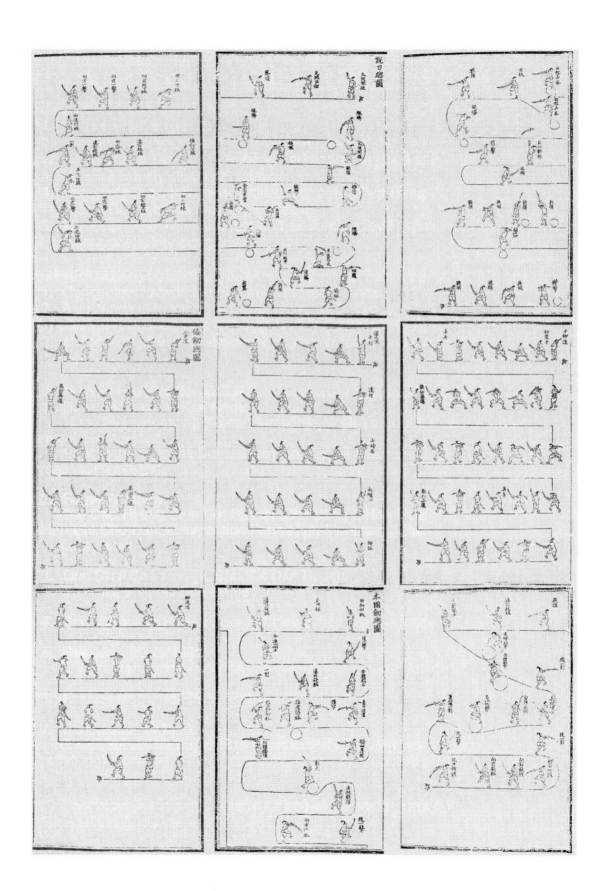

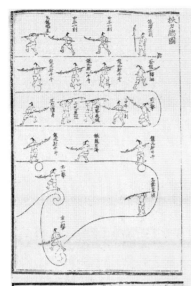

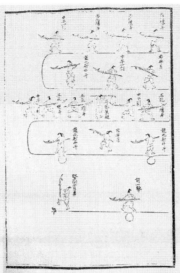

武藝圖譜通志卷之四

拳法

詩小雅無拳無勇職為亂階注拳力也爾雅疏

武編曰拳有勢者所以為變化也橫邪側面起立走伏皆有牆戶可以守可以攻故謂之勢拳有定勢而用無定勢當其用也變無定勢而實不失勢

茅元儀曰拳有勢者所以為變化也知拏跤而後可以拏跤而後可以馳驟者知此也八法書說曰王逸少書編工惯勤肢體為初學入藝之門

戚繼光曰拳法似無預于大戰之技然活動手足

少林王征南先生從學於單思南而獨得其全余嘗從學焉而其要則在乎鍊鍊既成熟不必顧盻擬合信手而應縱橫前後逢晷其鍊法有鍊手者三十五鍊步者十八而總攝於六路與十段錦之中各有歌訣其六路曰佃神通臂最為高斗門左右屯兵仙人立起朝天勢撒出抱月不相饒揚鞭左右人難及煞錘衝擄兩翅搖其十段錦曰立起坐山虎勢迴身急三追架刀斫歸營進步隨前進滾斫退歸原路入步韜隨前進滾斫歸

松溪為最

寧波府志曰少林法主于搏人而跳踉奮躍或失之疎故沿性為人所乘松溪之法主于禦敵非遇困厄不發發則所當必靡無隙可乘故內家之術尤善其搏人必以其穴有暈穴有啞穴有死穴相其穴而輕重擊之或死或暈或啞無毫髮爽其秘者有敬緊徑勁切五字訣非入室弟子不以相授蓋此五字不以為用而所以神其用猶兵家之仁信智勇嚴云

內家拳法曰自外家至少林其術精矣張三峯既精於少林復從而翻之是名內家得其一二者已足勝

虎徒搏也馮河徒涉也左傳晉矦夢與楚子搏即拳搏也又作卞漢書哀帝紀贊時覽卞射武戲注手搏為卞角力為武戲甘延壽以材力傳試弁手搏期門以金日磾力能扛鼎孫十三老其法起于宋之張三峯三峯為武當丹士徽宗召之道梗不得進夜夢玄帝授之拳法厥明以單丁殺賊百餘遂以絕技名世由三峯而後至嘉靖時傳於四明寧波府志

一為內家則少林為外家蓋此拳起於宋之張三峯松溪為正傳而

乳左足搶左右手徑左耳後向右前斫下鈎起閣左後右拗似朝天勢右足隨後鈎起右足當前橫向外靠左足尖如丁字樣是為仙人步凡步俱蹲坐直立者病法所禁把月右足至後大撒步右足隨轉斫右作坐馬步仍還連枝步左右手仍還斗門兩足搓右足搓拗前手還斗門右足斜前右足在前兩手仍四長拳煞右手掠右足搓轉向當前陰陽面右足在內兩脇夾脇煞雙左手撄左手扯右足仍左手陽發陰左足進同上然錘左足平

初飛步金雞獨立緊攢弓坐馬四平兩顧盻其詞皆隱略難記余因各為詮釋之六路曰斗門左垂右手衝上當前右手平屈向外一敵衝上右足隨前右足又隨左拳衝前連枝步通臂長拳也右手前斫隨前手以雙指從左拳鈎進復鈎出作小�步連枝隨還右拳皆衝立左拳亦隨右拳斫下亦伏

仙人朝天勢將左手長拳往右耳後向左前斫下伏右手伏乳右手伏乳其四長拳左足搓隨右拳左手長拳從右耳後向右前斫下指從左拳鈎進復鈎出右手

數勢之相連未必勢勢相承聯絡不斷如易之有序卦故茅氏論朝鮮劒勢亦分洗法刺法擊法而已我國銳刀既載茅說乃復習以俗譜卽以拳法言之感譜必兩兩相對如甲作探馬乙作拗單鞭甲作七星乙作騎龍之類皆攻守自然之勢而今法則初作某勢再作某勢從頭至尾湊成一通已失本意又況甲乙同作一勢如影隨形其相搏也不過雁翅丘劉數勢而終之兩相彝(數卷切 雙生子)負相撲而起此始近戲第其行之既久仍舊譜焉識者當自知之其十勢遂於今本故增入並錄其訣

面兩紐滾斫退歸原路左手翻身三斫退步蹈隨前進左手平著胸略撒開平直右手覆拳挽上至左手腕中止左足隨左手入斂步翻身右手亦平著胸同上滾斫歸初飛步右手斫後右足撻挪金雞立緊攀弓右手復斫右足撻轉左拳自上揷下左足釣馬進半步右足隨還連枝卽六路拳衝釣馬步坐馬四平兩顧卽六路兩翅搖擺還斗門轉坐馬搖擺六路與十段錦多相同處大約六路鍊骨使之能緊十段錦緊後又使之放開

[案]中國之二十四槍三十二拳隨機百變雖或有

在前仍爲連枝步而此用進退斂步循環三進雙刀斂步左膊垂下拳直竪當前右手平屈向外义左手內兩足緊斂步滾斫進退三廻將前手抹下後手斫進如是者三進三退凡斫法上圓中直下仍圓如鉞斧撬分身十字兩手仍著胸以左手撒開左足隨左手出右手出長拳循環三拳右手仍著胸以右手撒開左足轉面左手出長拳亦循環三拳架刀斫歸營寨右手復义左手內斫法同前滾斫法但轉面只三斫用右手轉身紐拳碾步拳下垂左手略出右手下出上進俱陰面左足隨左手右足垂右手摟挪不轉

仍作七星拳勢左右洗作高四平勢右手左脚前一刺

進前作懸脚虛餌勢右足蹴右手左足蹴左手右足蹴右手卽作順鸞肘勢左一廻左手一打右足

拳法譜

[總]兩人各以左右手夾腰雙立初作探馬勢右手打開左肩旋作拗鸞肘勢左手打開右肩

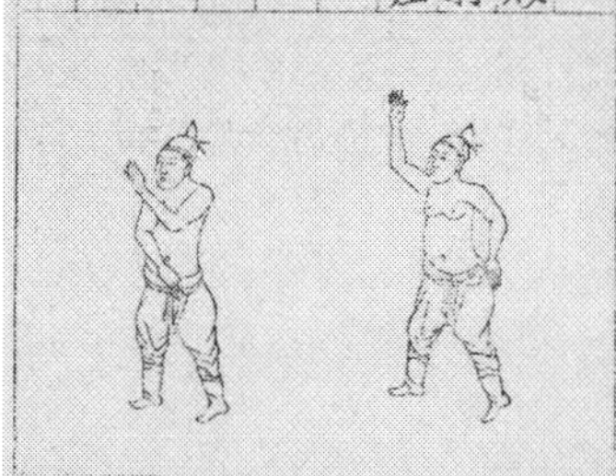

仍作下揷勢左一廻右手左足一打卽作當頭砲勢左手防前右手遮額

仍作拗單鞭勢跳一步右手打右臀仍作伏虎勢進坐右廻起立又作懸脚虛餌勢

卽作倒揷勢左右手高擧後顧回身向後作一霎步勢右手夾右腋

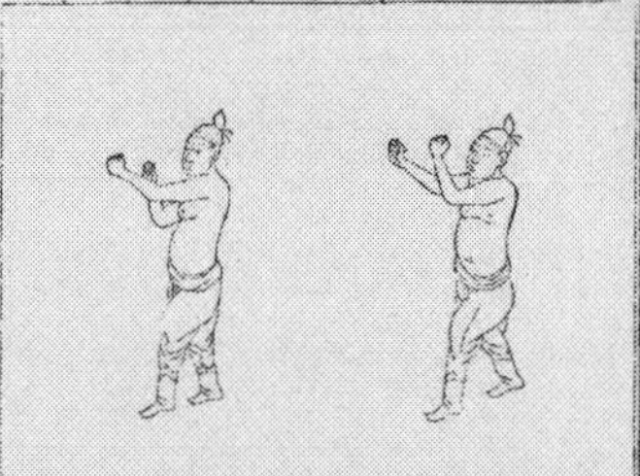

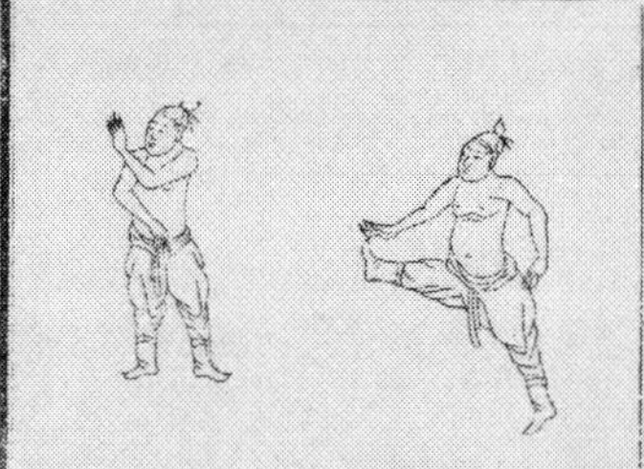

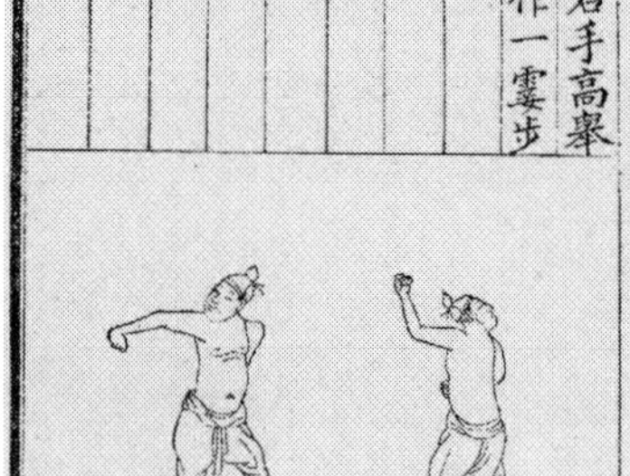

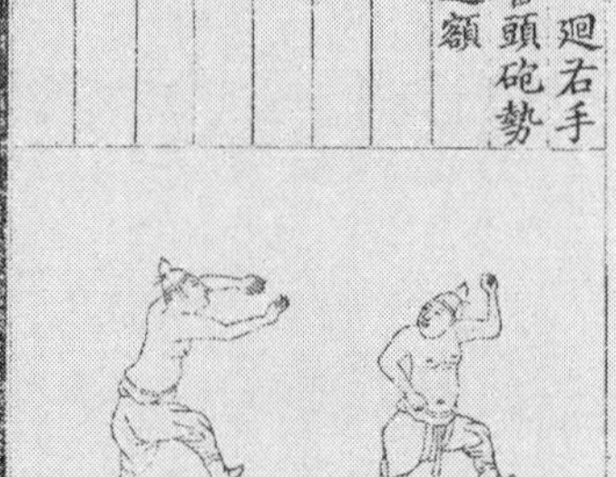

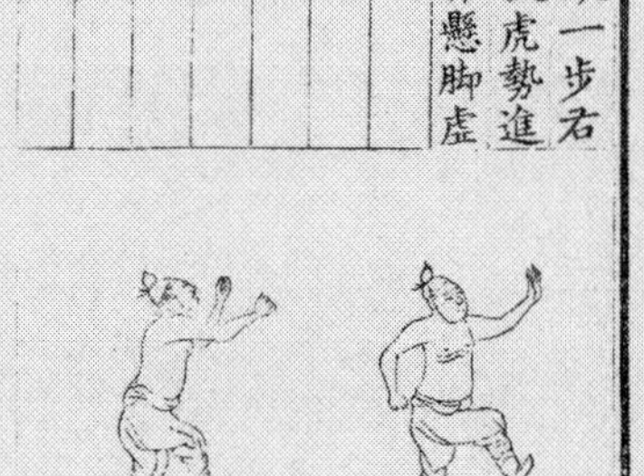

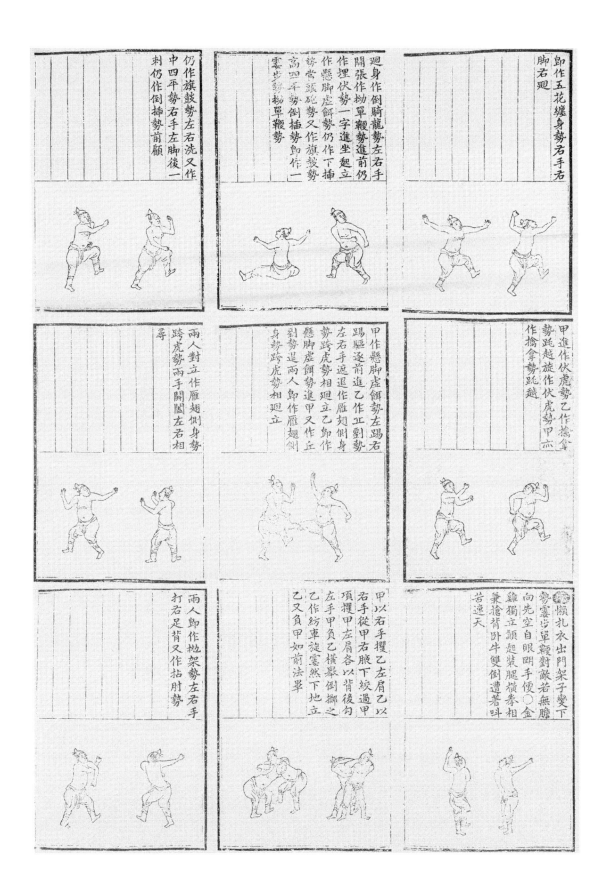

8. Hwa Rang World Tang Soo Do Lineage

Welcome to the Hwa Rang World Tang Soo Do Moo Duk Kwan Federation. I am pleased that you have decided to pursue the traditional martial art of Tang Soo Do, and wish you the best in your endeavors.

I formed the Hwa Rang Federation in 1994 because I saw the necessity of an association that not only emphasized Tang Soo Do technique, but the virtues of faithfulness, perseverance, and honesty as well. My wish for my students and the members of this federation is that they will not only grow in their Tang Soo Do Technique, but also in their personal and spiritual lives. We are seeking to develop the body in conjunction with the mind, not for its own sake, but for the benefit for others. When one has good physical and mental health, he or she can be more dedicated to the family, the Nation, and even the World. Tang Soo Do can and should be a way of thought and life, in which one puts aside himself for the good of everyone around him.

Tang Soo Do is not a sport. Though it is not essentially competitive, it has great combat applications. As a classical martial art, its purpose is to develop every aspect of the self, in order to create a mature person who totally integrates his/her intellect, body, emotions, and spirit. This integration helps to create a person who is free from inner conflict and who can deal with the outside world.

I can only guide you in your study of Tang Soo Do. In the end, it is you that will achieve your goals. If you want to be a "Great Warrior", you must be willing to sacrifice the time and effort to reach it. Do not just attend class, but analyze the techniques, dissect the movements. "Perfect practice makes perfect," and perfection only comes if you work for it. If you are willing to dedicate yourself to the study of Tang Soo Do, you will reap the physical, spiritual, and mental benefits that come along with it.

Best wishes,

Grand Master Ho Sik Pak
January 2000

LINEAGE
Grand Master Pak Ho Sik
Grand Master Lee Pal Young
Grand Master Hong Jong Soo
Grand Master Hwang Kee
Grand Master Yang Ku Chin

9. 10 Key Concepts

1. Yong Gi .... Courage
2. In Neh .... Endurance
3. Chung Shin Tong Il .... Concentration
4. Chung Jik .... Honesty
5. Kyum Son .... Humility
6. Him Cho Chung .... Control of Power
7. Shin Chook .... Tension and Relaxation
8. Wan Gup .... Speed Control
9. Jung Uei .... Justice
10. Uei Rhee .... Best Friendship

10 Articles of Faith

1. Be loyal to one's country: Sacrifice to fulfill your duty to your country and your people. This is based on the spirit of Hwa Rang.
2. Be obedient to ones parents and elders: Children should be dutiful to their parents and parents should be charitable to their children.
3. Be loving to one's husband and wife: From the mother's body develops man's happiness, as harmony and affection from love between the sexes.
4. Be cooperative to your brothers: Hold together with cooperation and concord.
5. Be respectful to elders: Protect the right of the weak with courtesy and modesty.
6. Be faithful to your teacher: Learn truth through the practice of duty, loyalty, and affection.
7. Be faithful to friends: Honor friendship and be peaceful and happy with harmony and faith towards all mankind.
8. Kill only in justice and with honor: Be able to distinguish between good and bad with fairness and rightfulness.
9. Never retreat in battle: Sacrifice for justice with capability and bravery.
10. Always finish what you start: Move to action with sureness and with hope.

Student Creed

1. To build true confidence through knowledge in the mind, honesty in the heart, and strength in the body.
2. To keep friendship with one another and build a strong and happy community.
3. Never fight to achieve selfish ends, but to develop might for right.

10. Hand & Foot Targeting Areas

● Methods of Attack

In Tang Soo Do certain areas of the body are used as weapons. Indeed, many times the entire body is considered a weapon. If this notion is given full consideration, then any portion of the body should be thought of in a different way. Certain parts of the body are used as weapons mainly because they are easy to direct, less vulnerable to attack or are harder than other parts of the body. When thinking about what a weapon ought to do, one must also be self-reflective and consider if their body could be thought of as a weapon. Many times the body needs conditioning to be thought of as a weapon. Although conditioning can take on many forms, in this context "conditioning" is associated with the hardening of the weapon (body, arm, or hand).

In this section the uses of various body parts as weapons will be explained along with appropriate striking zones for each of them.

● Ball of the Foot

This weapon is used as an alternative to the instep of the foot. There are two ways to use ball of the foot. One way is with the foot pointed at the target with the toes pulled back. This formation is used primarily for all types of front kicks except the front snap kick. The second way to use the ball of the foot is with the foot flexed and the toes pulled back. Using the foot like this provides a second way to perform a more powerful round-house kick to reach around some of the opponent's blocks. You must be more accurate with these techniques because the ball of the foot is a small area used to attack; and using the ball of the foot shortens the distance of techniques used with it.

Front Thrust Kick with ball of the foot (*Ap Cha Nuk Ki*)

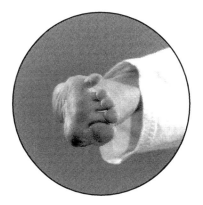

Round House Kick to face with ball of the foot

● Instep of Foot

The instep is located on top of the foot. Techniques using it are normally the "round house" kick and "front snap" kick. When using the instep for a technique, it is important to point the foot completely and pull the toes down. Pointing the foot allows muscles in the instep to harden exposing a bone thus increasing the effectiveness of an instep kick. Pulling back the toes down protects them from potential injury while performing a technique.

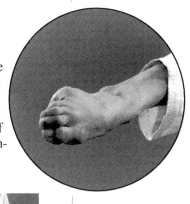

Front Snap Kick
to groin with instep

Round house Kick (*Ap Dollyo Cha Ki*) using instep

● Back of the heel

The back of the heel is located at the rear of the foot just below the "Achilles tendon". It is normally used in attacks like "hook kicks" and "axe kicks". To use this technique the foot must be flexed in a right angle with the toes pulled back. When the foot is flexed this hardens the heel and readies it for attack. Sometimes the back of the heel is used in conjunction with the side of the foot called the "knife-edge". One technique that this is used in is the "crescent kick".

  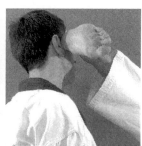

Kick to Groin with heel   Axe Kick to face or Shoulder   Hook Kick to Head
with heel

● Bottom of the foot

This weapon can be used as an alternative to the back of the heel. To use this weapon the foot must be pointed with the bottom of the foot prepared for impact. This weapon is mainly used in hook kick attacks. It is only in recent history that this weapon has been accepted as effective in real combat. Before only the heel was considered strong enough, but with the advent of point sparring the bottom of the foot is now considered adequate. Even though it is not as strong as the heel it has a greater reaching distance and is still effective in combat situations.

Hook Kick with bottom of foot (*Kok Kwang Ee Cha Ki*)

Knee

When using the knee as a weapon, be sure to bend it as much as possible. By bending it, the hardest part of the knee is exposed, making it useful for all knee kicks. A knee kick can be done in a roundhouse or forward thrusting motion. Sometimes a knee kick is done with the foot flexed, but by leaving the toes pointed it allows more energy to be channeled to the knee itself. Because of the nature of knee techniques they are generally done in close combat situations.

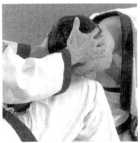

Knee Kicks (*Moorup Cha Ki*) to face

Side of the heel and foot

The formation of this weapon is very similar to the back of the heel. The foot is flexed in a right angle with the toes pulled back. The only difference is its application. The bottom of the heel and the side of the foot are ideal for use in "side kicks" and "back kicks". Although the side of the foot is also used, the bottom of the heel is the primary point that will impact the target.

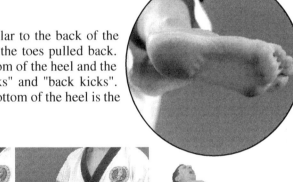

Side Kicks (*Yup Cha Ki*) to face and body using the edge of the heel and foot

Middle Punch (*Jung Kwon*) - Fist

The middle punch is the most common of all the attacking techniques. It is formed by tightly curling the fingers into the palm then wrapping the thumb over the fingers to hold the fingers in place. When using this technique it's important to focus on the first and second knuckles as the points to attack with. This position aligns the bones in the wrist and the arm, providing support for the technique. Focusing on only two knuckles concentrates energy to create more force and damage. When used as a back fist, the top of the knuckles are used instead of their front at the fist as in the straight punch.

► How to make a fist

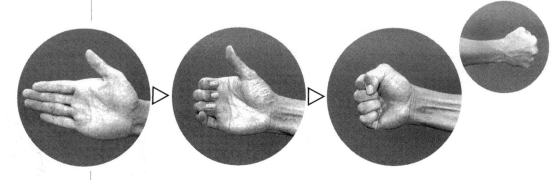

► Applications

Middle punch to solar plexus   Back Fist to bridge of nose   Middle punch to bridge of nose

Back Fist to temple

First Knuckle Punch (*Il ji kwon*)

This weapon is formed by making a regular fist while exposing the first knuckle. The thumb should be placed in such a way that it supports the first knuckle. Clenching the fist allows the first knuckle to cement in place preparing it for attack. This weapon is used to attack some of the smaller vital points of the body. It also requires more precision when applied. To increase the effectiveness of this attack conditioning should be done to harden this softer weapon.

Middle Knuckle Punch (*E ji kwon*)

As in the "First Knuckle Punch" the knuckle is exposed and the fist is clenched tightly, only in this case the middle knuckle is exposed. This hand position is more "fightable" than the first knuckle punch. This is because its position is easier to hold. Again conditioning would increase the effectiveness of this weapon.

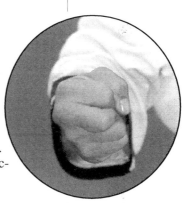

One Finger Strike (*Il ji kwon soo*)

This weapon is based on the "spear-hand" formation. It is formed by putting the hand in "spear-hand" formation extending the index finger and pulling the other fingers back at the middle knuckles. This weapon is most effective in attacks to the eyes or throat. Using this weapon in other areas that are not as vulnerable would require more conditioning.

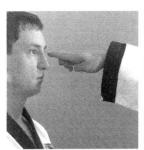

Two Finger Strike (*E ji kwon soo*)

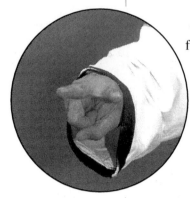

This weapon is also based on the "spear-hand" formation. It is formed by splitting the index and the middle finger, and using the rest of the fingers for support. Notice that the index finger and the middle finger are in-line with the bones in the hand and the arm, this is to give added strength to the technique. It is ideal for attacks to the eyes.

Plier Hand Strike (*Jip kye son kong kyuk*)

This weapon is formed by cupping the hands just as if to grab something. The only difference is that the hand should be firm and ready to be used as a striking technique. When applied the hand actually strikes the neck first, then holding on to choke the opponent.

Wrist Strike (*Dung Joo Mock*)

This weapon is ideal for quick transitions from blocks to attacks, often being used in conjunction with the palm strike. To form this weapon bend the wrist forward so that it is fully exposed and bring the fingers together so that they are all touching. It is good for attacking nearly every part of the body.

Palm Strike (Jang Kwon Kong Kyuk)

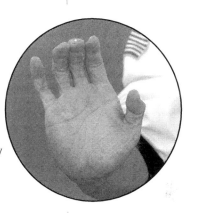

This weapon is formed by pulling the wrist and fingers back. The portion of the hand used to strike is the heel of the palm and the "knife edge" of the hand. Sometimes when applied to face attacks, the fingers are kept limp, thus allowing the fingers to flicker into or scratch the eyes. Generally it is good for attacking the face and body areas.

Ridge Hand (Yuk Soo Do Kong Kyuk)

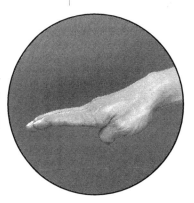

This weapon is one of the trademarks of Tang Soo Do. The "spear-hand" is formed by bending the fingers slightly, then pulling the thumb underneath the hand. The inside edge of the hand is used for striking. When the thumb is pulled underneath the hand, the bones in the hand form a triangular shape; this is the point to strike with.

Knife Hand (*Soo Do*)

The knife hand is another trademark move in Tang Soo Do. It formed by pulling the fingers together and finally pulling the middle finger in to match levels with the first and ring finger. Make sure the thumb is not sticking out, and also make sure the wrist is supporting the rest of the hand. It is useful for quick exchanges between blocks and attacks. When attacking the "knife-edge" of the hand is used, but when applied in a block the wrist is used. Often when applied as a block, the wrist is slightly bent this is to make the opponent's attack easier to grab and parry. This weapon is good for most attacks to the face and some areas of the body.

▶ How to make a knife Hand (*Soo Do*)

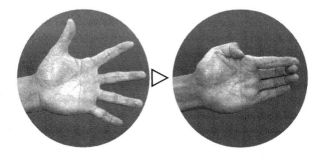

● Elbow Strike (*Pal Koop*)

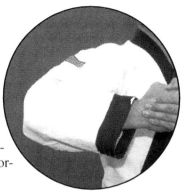

This weapon is used primarily is close combat situations. It is formed by bending the elbow completely and exposing one of the hardest bones of the body. Sometimes the other hand is used to support the attack but this depends on the type of elbow strike. When striking, the tip of the elbow is not actually the point used to strike with, it is actually the part just below the point or above. It is good for attacks to any portion of the body, but most effective when applied to the face or body.

11. Stances

Joon Bee and Ba Ro Stances

Joon Bee Jaseh is done before the beginning and end (*Ba Ro Jaseh*) of various techniques like the forms (*hyungs*) or one-step sparring. Look straight forward, chin is inward. Your focus should be directly ahead with your thoughts on the techniques you are about to perform. You are preparing mentally, physically and spiritually.

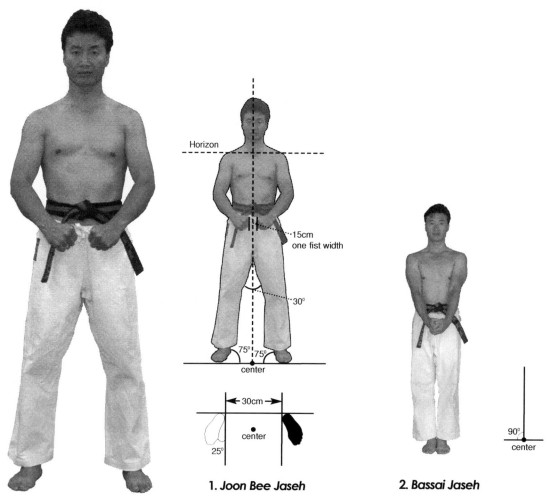

1. Joon Bee Jaseh

2. Bassai Jaseh

3. *Nai Han Chi Jaseh*

4. *Sip Soo Jaseh*

5. *Kong San Kun Jaseh*

6. *Wan Shu Jaseh*

7. *Dam Dwai Jaseh*

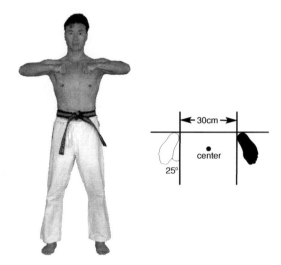

8. So Rim Jang Kwon Jaseh

9. Kyo Cha Rip Jaseh

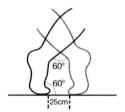

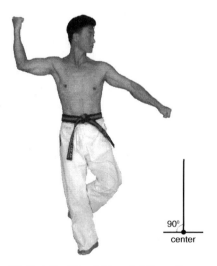

10. Hak Dari Seoki Jaseh (Crane)

● Major Stances

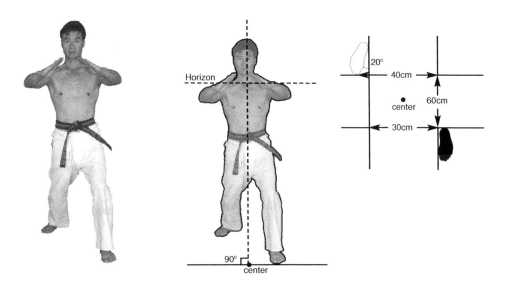

1. Front *(Jun Gul)* Jaseh

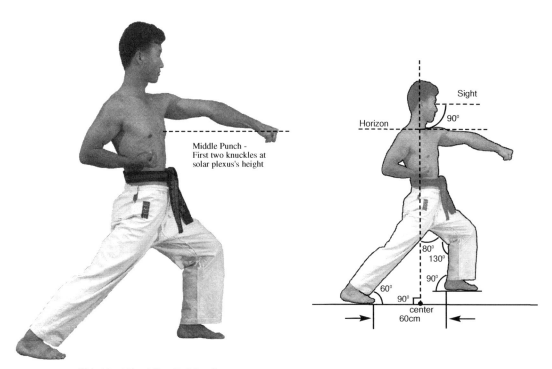

(Side View) *Front (Jun Gul) Jaseh*

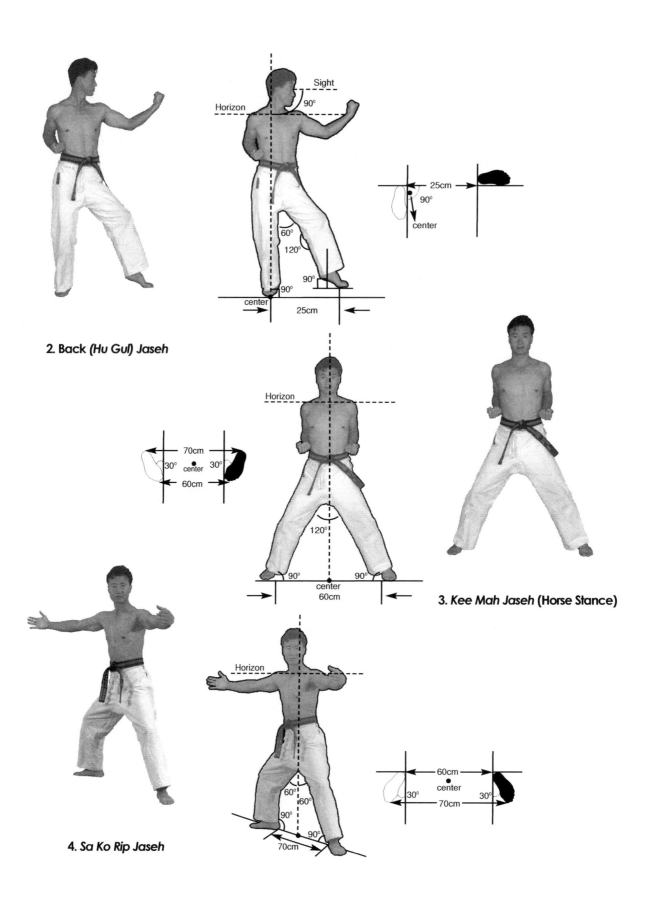

2. Back (Hu Gul) Jaseh

3. Kee Mah Jaseh (Horse Stance)

4. Sa Ko Rip Jaseh

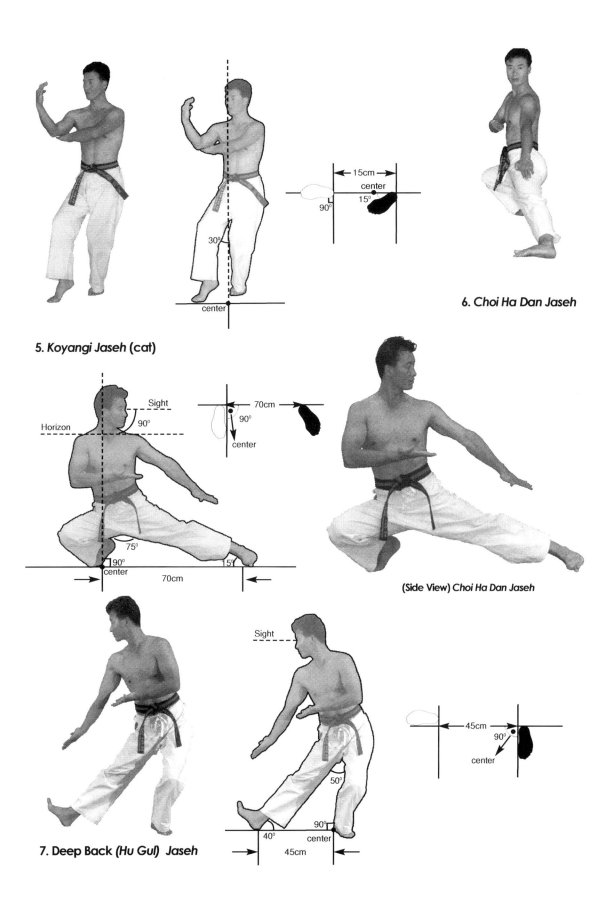

6. Choi Ha Dan Jaseh

5. Koyangi Jaseh (cat)

(Side View) *Choi Ha Dan Jaseh*

7. Deep Back (*Hu Gul*) Jaseh

12. Hip Turns

● Defensive Hip & Offensive Hip

Of all of the different types of martial arts, Tang Soo Doo, above any other, stresses the importance of the use of the *Her Ri*. *Her Ri* translated into English means "the waist" or "the hip". The *Her Ri* is located in the center of body, it marks the division between upper and lower body. For this reason it is important to pay attention to its importance. Because it is located in the middle, it plays a significant role in how it controls the body's motion. The major motions in Tang Soo Do consist of offensive and defensive movements. These two separate functions each have individual hip turns. Some of the other functions of the *Her Ri* that contribute to the value of the offense and defense are often taken for granted. These contributing functions are balance, speed and power. When these functions of the hip are fine tuned, each offensive and defensive motion will increase in power.

When thinking about a simple function such as walking, every step is directed by a movement in the hips. Not only that, the hips force the arms to swing into place, balancing the rest of the body perfectly. When walking, try moving the arms so that they move in the same direction as the legs. This looks funny, creating an imbalance in the body's movements. In this case, the twisting of the hip is conflicting with the motion of the arms and will eventually cause back pain and fatigue. There are ways, however, to move the legs in the same direction as the arms; this will be explained later. Regardless of some difficult movements in Tang Soo Do, techniques generally follow the natural movements of the human body. These movements are achieved by using the hip to balance, coordinate, and lead the motion.

Every technique has its intention. Whether a technique is directed low or high, or directed at the ribs or the solar plexus; to achieve proper balance it is necessary to direct the hip motion in the same direction as the technique. When done correctly, maximum efficiency will be achieved. Speed will increase along with balance and power.

A person can only walk as fast as their hips are able to move. In the same respect a person can only do a technique as fast as their hips can move. It is impossible to run while moving the arms and hip at a slow rate. Along with speed, the hip is also used to create power. An important physics equation tells us that Velocity multiplied by Mass equals Force. By using hip movement in every technique a person uses the entire body in every technique.

As explained earlier the hip motion forces the rest of the body into motion while walking. It only seems logical to capitalize on this fact by using the hip to incorporate the entire body to perform techniques. This will create natural speed and power. By performing a technique using the entire body, it creates the opportunity to generate optimal power as long as sufficient speed is used.

The *Her Ri* is a vital component of the body to pay attention to while training in Tang Soo Do. As the center of the body, it is responsible for directing the rest of the body. A notable quote from Grand Master Hwang Kee is "The will is in the waist", it is an excerpt from his poem *Sip Sam Se*. Meaning the will is the intention of the technique guided by the waist (Hip). Balance will increase with the natural use of the hip. Speed will increase, and with speed power, as the hip is responsible for guiding the entire body into the technique.

• Defensive Hip Turn

| Beginning Motion | Intermediate Motion | Complete Motion |

There are two major ways to use the hip, defensive and offensive. These motions are designed to help the effectiveness of each technique. As a rule, most defensive techniques will use the defensive hip turn and most offensive techniques will use the offensive hip turn. There are exceptions that are commonly used but if all the motions possible are taken into account, the rule is fairly steadfast.

The defensive hip turn, also commonly called "toe to toe" or "toe to heel", is exactly that. In the first set of photos, Grand Master Pak is completing a "low block" using a defensive hip turn. In the first photo he is bringing his left foot toward the toe of his right foot. In the next photo he steps out with the left foot in a circular motion, but has not yet turned the hip all the way over, nor has he extended his arm out to block. In the next photo the technique is complete with his hip fully turned over into "Front Stance".

• Offensive Hip Turn

Beginning Motion   Intermediate Motion   Complete Motion

Just like the defensive hip turn, the offensive hip turn is commonly called by what it is, "heel to heel". Here he is shown completing a middle punch. In the first photo Grand Master Pak draws the heel of the right foot toward the heel of the left foot and the toes are pointed to the outside of the body. In the next photo he steps out further, almost all the way, but his hip is not turned over, nor is his technique complete. In the final photo the punch is complete, with the hip fully turned over into "front stance."

When performing any technique it is important to use a proper, complete hip motion. Notice that in each case, both defensive and offensive, Grand Master Pak doesn't complete the hip motion until the very final moment. Although he is stepping forward, his hip is still pulled back along with his technique. The only reason this is done is to create power in the technique. By using the hip to direct the entire body, maximum power is achieved at final moment.

13. Rules of Rotation: Blocks & Strikes

Rotating your body by using the hips in a defensive block or offensive strike will generate much more power than only using your arms from a stationary position. When initiating a block or punch, first start with the hips open outward just before delivering the move, essentially cocking the body like a spring. Then drive the whole body into the move by rotating the hips around 90° inward. This action will generate your maximum power, using many of the muscle groups in your arm, side of the body, and leg. Not doing this technique only results in using your arm muscles, thus cheating yourself of much potential power.

In the illustrations below, all the blocks and strikes are initiated with the feet together with the body side-on to the opponent. This is the preparatory move. Then the whole body shifts into the final stance while strongly rotating the hips and delivering the block or strike.

• Examples of rotating the body into the delivery of blocks and strikes

Rotating into a two fist middle block, *Jun Gul Ssang Soo Ahneso Phakuro Mahk Kee*, forward stance.

Rotating into a high block, *Sang Dan Mahk Kee*, forward stance.

Rotating into a side punch in horse stance, *Wheng Jin Kong Kyuk*.

14. "180° Rules"

Like hip rotation, the "180° Rule" is used to obtain maximum power in a block or strike by using more of the body's muscles and force. When initiating a move, first chamber or begin the block or hit on the opposite side of the body from where the move will end. Execute the block or punch so that when the move is complete, the final position of the hand and arm should be about 180° from its origin. Powerful blocks and strikes can be made when applying "180° rule" together with hip rotation discussed in the previous section.

Beginning Motion

Ha Dan Soo Do Mahk Kee

Choi Ha Dan Soo Do Mahk Kee

Beginning Motion

Sang Dan Soo Do Mahk Kee

Jung Dan Soo Do Mahk Kee

Tuel Uh Yuk Jin Kong Kyuk

Tuel Uh Kwan Soo Kong Kyuk

Beginning Motion

Tuel Uh Pal Gup Kong Kyuk

Beginning Motion

Ssang Soo Sang Dan Mahk Kee
(open hand)

Ssang Soo Sang Dan Mahk Kee

Ssang Soo Ha Dan Mahk Kee

15. Vital Areas: Front & Back

• Striking Points explained

The striking points laid out in the following diagrams point out most of the vital points on the human body. These points are specific striking zones, many of which consist of only a square inch of space. Some of them may be obvious; others are a result of years of trial and error and lengthy research. These points vary in how vital they are. The throat for example is one the most vital points on the body. By hitting the throat, passage of air may be stopped; the result is suffocation. Other points like the calf or parts of the arm are useful for disabling an opponent but not killing an opponent. The side of the neck is targeted because it is where the jugular artery is located. Other places like the top of the shoulder are chosen because that is where a nerve junction is located and will cause extreme pain if hit correctly. Another pressure point is the side of outer thigh, because it is where two major muscles come together. If they are hit at their meeting place the result is a pain that could best be described in English as a "Charley Horse". Other places are just not protected very well: one example is the solar plexus.

Because many of these points are small, it is obvious that hitting them correctly requires "pin point" accuracy. Not only that, but the direction of intention is important too. What this means, is to aim for a specific place not just for a general area. By doing this, power is directed specifically not generally, creating a greater impact on the target.

● Striking Points

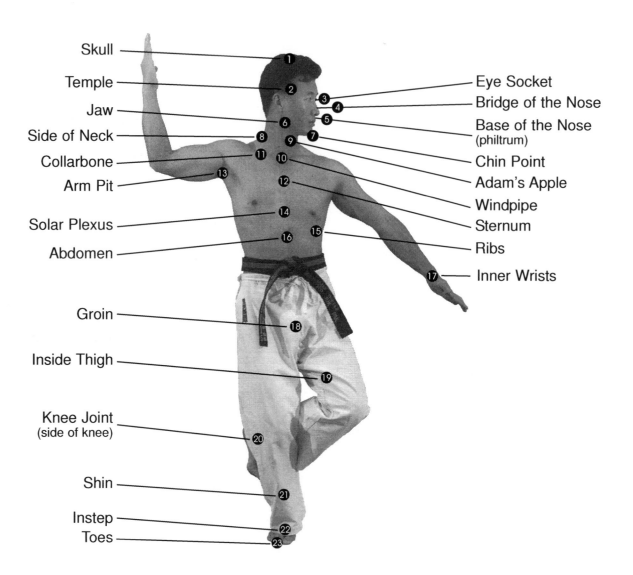

Skull — ①

Temple — ②

Jaw — ⑥

Side of Neck — ⑧

Collarbone — ⑪

Arm Pit — ⑬

Solar Plexus — ⑭

Abdomen — ⑯

Groin — ⑱

Inside Thigh — ⑲

Knee Joint (side of knee) — ⑳

Shin — ㉑

Instep — ㉒

Toes — ㉓

③ — Eye Socket

④ — Bridge of the Nose

⑤ — Base of the Nose (philtrum)

⑩ — Chin Point

⑨ — Adam's Apple

⑦ — Windpipe

⑫ — Sternum

⑮ — Ribs

⑰ — Inner Wrists

● Techniques and Striking Points used

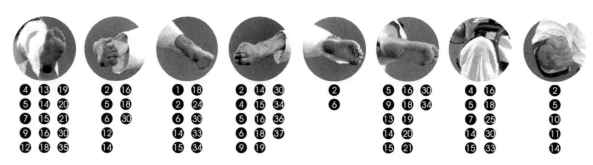

④ ⑬ ⑲	② ⑯	① ⑱	② ⑭ ㉚	②	⑤ ⑯ ㉚	④ ⑯	②
⑤ ⑭ ⑳	⑤ ⑱	② ㉔	④ ⑮ ㉞	⑥	⑨ ⑱ ㉞	⑤ ⑱	⑤
⑦ ⑮ ㉑	⑥ ㉚	⑥ ㉚	⑤ ⑯ ㊱		⑬ ⑲	⑦ ㉕	⑩
⑨ ⑯ ㉚	⑫	⑭ ㉝	⑥ ⑱ ㊲		⑭ ⑳	⑭ ㉚	⑪
⑫ ⑱ ㉟	⑭	⑮ ㉞	⑨ ⑲		⑮ ㉑	⑮ ㉝	⑭

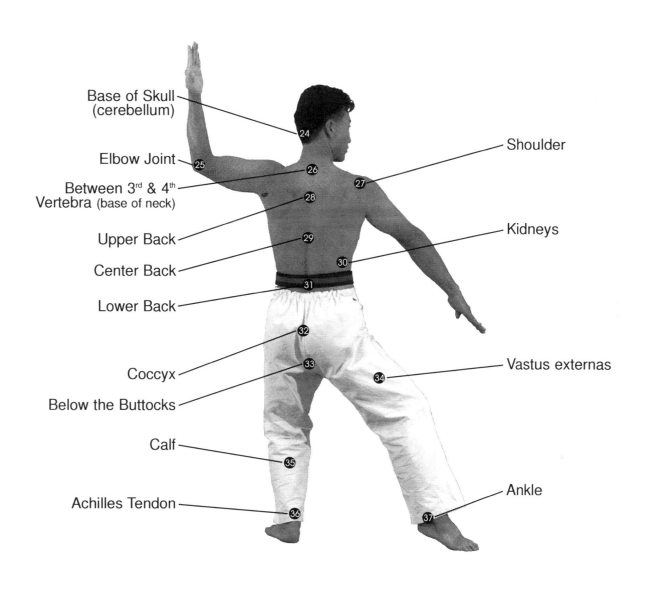

Base of Skull (cerebellum) — 24

Elbow Joint — 25

Between 3rd & 4th Vertebra (base of neck) — 26

Upper Back — 28

Center Back — 29

Lower Back — 31

Coccyx — 32

Below the Buttocks — 33

Calf — 35

Achilles Tendon — 36

Shoulder — 27

Kidneys — 30

Vastus externas — 34

Ankle — 37

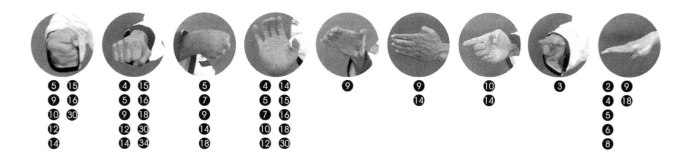

5 15	4 15	5	4 14	9	9	10	3	2 9
9 16	5 16	7	5 15		14	14		4 18
10 30	9 18	9	7 16					5
12	12 30	14	10 18					6
14	14 34	18	12 30					8

⑯ Basic Warm Up

Always warm up and stretch every training session. The importance of this sort of preparation cannot be overstressed. By increasing stretching the ability to perform difficult kicks also increases. It also helps to prevent against all types of injury especially form over-extension. Stretching is a continual process and must be continually improved upon and maintained.

Prior to stretching is necessary to warm up your muscles. Incorporating a light jog or a set of jumping jacks prepares the body for a more intense workout.

Remember warm up and stretching is usually a quiet time that can be used to meditate on the subsequent workout.

Guidelines for stretching:	Benefits of Stretching:
- Do not rush. Always move Slowly, with control. - Don't Bounce. - Stretch until you feel some tension in the muscle (not the joint), and hold it comfortably for the time recommended. - Don't overstretch. Overstretching can lower the level of flexibility. - Do not bend from your lower back, but from the hip. - Don't hold your breath. Remember to breath while stretching. - You should never feel pain while stretching, only some discomfort.	**- Stretching prior to exercise will reduce chances of injuries.** **- Stretching at the end of a work out will improve flexibility.** - Prevent and alleviates muscle soreness after exercise. - Improves coordination, performance and posture. - Reduces lower back pain. - Increases blood flow to the body. - Increases the functional range of motion.

Cool down by slowly reducing the intensity of the work out. Follow up by stretching again. This is the best time to improve flexibility. Focus especially on stretching the muscles most used during training.

❶ Spread your legs as wide as you can. Keep your knees straight, heels extended. Start by massaging the muscles of the inner thigh using a 'Knife hand' (*Soo Do*, pg 44). This will help blood circulation and loosing up the legs.

❷ Bring one leg in front extended out and bend the other leg across the top of it. Grab your foot and rotate your ankle slowly and with control to warm it up. Rotate in both directions.

❸ While leaving one leg extended out, lift the other one up using your hand. Keep both knees from bending. The opposite hand holds the foot in a flexed position "turned in".

❹ For more advanced students bring the other hand at the ankle lifting the leg as high as possible. This will help you stretch further, but remember to keep the knees from bending. Hold in this position for at least ten seconds. Repeat steps 2 - 4 on the other side.

❺ In this position, one leg is extended out and the other leg is bent across the top of it. Hold the knee with one hand and the foot with the other. This is preparation for the next exercise.

❻ In this position bend the body over and bring the chest to the knee. Hold for at least ten seconds. Repeat steps 5 and 6 on the other side.

❼ Extend one leg to the side, and bend the other one in bringing your heel to your groin. Start by moving forward from your hip and catching your foot with both hands. Bend the entire body over, resting your abdomen, chest and finally your head on your shin. Hold for as long as is comfortable.

7. If you have tight hamstrings and can't catch your foot, try looping your belt around it. Bend forward from the lower back. Be careful not to try bringing your head to your thighs, but your chest instead, lengthening the spine.

❽ Breathe in, release gently and breathe out. Breathe in again and reach over the other leg while breathing out. Hold as long as is comfortable. Repeat steps 7 and 8 on the other side.

❾ This time one leg is tucked in behind the body. Start out by bending from your hips and reaching out with both hands to catch the foot. While breathing out, relax your shoulder and arms and let your body bend forward slowly. Relax and hold.

❿ Without moving the position of the legs, come up, breathe in, and while breathing out reach over the bent leg. Be gentle if you've had knee injury. Relax and hold for a few seconds.

11. This is a great stretch after stomach exercises and after sitting or lifting for a long time.

❶❶ Lie on the floor on your stomach. While breathing out slowly lift your trunk, straightening your arms and knees. Curve your upper back, and hold in the upper position for 10 seconds. Repeat by first releasing the stretch. Breathe in lifting up your body again, and breathe out slowly allowing the back and stomach muscles to stretch further.

❶❷ In this same position slowly turn the body to one side and hold. Slowly reverse directions and turn to the other side. This is a great lower-back stretch.

❶❸ This exercise begins while lying flat on the stomach. Reach back with both arms to grab your feet. Making sure the stomach is flexed; pull the legs up and inwards curving the spine. Repeat several times to warm up, then hold up for as long as is comfortable. This stretch helps increase flexibility in the back and stomach.

❶❹ Begin by lying on the stomach and keeping both hands on the ground for stabilization and head support. Proceed to twist the spine and hip bringing one leg to the other side. The leg on the bottom should be extended out, and the leg on top should be bent. In this position relax the entire body and allow the force of gravity to stretch the back and spine. Hold for 10 seconds. Repeat on the other side.

❶❺ This exercise begins while lying on the back and leaving one leg extended out. Lift the other knee up into the chest and up towards the shoulder. Use both hands to hold the knee down relaxing the rest of the body. This action stretches the muscles in the hip and the top of the thigh. Hold in this position for several seconds. Repeat on both sides.

🄰 This exercise begins while lying on the back. Using both hands, pull your knees into the chest and up towards the shoulder. While in this position rock back and forth. This motion helps stretch the lower back muscles. A good variation is to rock sideways alternating sides. Also try not letting your feet touch the floor each time you come up to exercise your abdominal muscles.

🄱 Begin this motion while standing with the feet slightly wider than the shoulders. Reach down and touch the ground with the palms of your hands.

🄲 In the same position reach down and touch the elbows to the ground.

🄳 Come back bringing the hands on the hips.

🄴 And lean back stretching while using the hands to support the lower back and push the hips forward. Repeat steps 17-20 four times.

🄵 Begin this motion while standing with the feet slightly wider than the shoulders and the arms extended out to both sides. Reach down with the right hand, and touch the left foot while extending the opposite hand to the back creating a 180° line with the arms. Repeat this motion quickly while alternating from right to left at least ten times. ■

17. Kicks - *Cha Gi*

One of the hallmarks of Tang Soo Do are the array of kicks, ranging from quick snapping front-kicks to powerful jumping spinning back-kicks. Shown below is a series of the basic kicks - front, side, round-house, back, and crescents, with points about their execution. Virtually all kicks have three things in common:

❶ Always initiate the kick by bringing your knee up to "chamber" the kick, aiming at your target.

❷ Reach with your kick using your hips and lower body to achieve maximum distance and power while maintaining proper posture (i.e. straight back, well balanced, hands up in defensive position).

❸ After executing the kick, quickly snap the leg back to prepare for the next move and also preventing your opponent from grabbing it.

FRONT THRUST - AHP CHA NUT GI

- Strike with the ball of the foot, pulling the toes back.
- Thrust forward with the hips for maximum thrust and reach.
- Primary target is the opponent's solar plexus.

FRONT SNAP - AHP CHA GI

- Same as front thrust kick, but strike with top of foot using a snapping motion.
- Good kick for delivering strikes to groin, or face if opponent's head is low to the ground.

FRONT OBLIQUE - BIT CHA GI

- Initiate kick same as the front thrust, but about half way through, bend the trajectory of the kicking-path to the outside.
- Strike with ball of foot to opponent's upper body and face.
- Executed to slip through opponent's defenses to deliver strike to face.

SIDE - YUP CHA NUT GI

- "Chamber" foot close to knee of opposite keg.
- Snap leg out while rotating hips over, pulling buttocks in to align body in direction of kick.
- Kick with the outer edge and heel of the foot.
- Use to deliver powerful kicks to opponent's torso and head.

SIDE HOOK – YUP HU RI GI

- Bring leg up as in first part of the side kick, then hook across target with heel or bottom of foot.
- Path of hooking motion should be parallel with ground.
- Used for quick, powerful strike to head.

ROUND HOUSE – AHP DOLL RYO CHA GI

- After bringing knee up, execute kick by thrusting out and rolling hips over.
- Kick with top of foot or ball of foot, reaching for target.
- Good kick for striking opponent's leg, knee, thigh, ribs, and head.

SPINNING BACK – DWI CHA GI

- When facing target, turn clockwise while picking-up trailing leg for kick. Look over shoulder to spot target, then thrust straight back into target.
- Conclude by rotating 360° to bring kicking leg back into the same position
- from which you initiated the kick.
- Very effective kick to strike opponent's solar plexus while protecting your body.

INSIDE TO OUTSIDE - AHNESO PHAKURO CHA GI

- Swing your foot from inside to outside opponent's body.
- Kick with the back of your heel.
- Be sure to bring foot above target to create momentum.
- Use for striking top of head, shoulder, face or chest.

● Jump Kicks

Spectacular jumping kicks are one of the hallmarks of Korean Martial Arts. Legend has it that jumping kicks, particularly the Jump Side Kick, were used to knock horsemen from their mounts. Illustrated below are some of the main jump kicks used in Tang Soo Do.

JUMP FRONT KICK

- Initiate by thrusting the knee of one leg up to gain momentum, then kicking with the opposite leg.
- This kick can be used to quickly cover distance and launch an attack at an opponents chest and head.

JUMP OBLIQUE FRONT KICK

- Same as the Jump Front Kick, but ball of foot is thrust obliquely to the outside.
- Used to slip under blocks when attacking the head.

JUMP BACK KICK

- When jumping up, first look over shoulder to spot target, then kick out with leg.
- A Jump Spinning Back Kick is delivered when you jump up, rotating 180° and kicking with the rear leg.
- This is a powerful kick to use while protecting the front of your body.

JUMP ROUND KICK

- The Jump Round-house can be executed as a regular kick with the front leg or spinning-style using the rear leg (as illustrated).
- After launching the kick, roll hips over to properly hit target with the top of the foot.

JUMP SIDE KICK

- Like the Round-house, the Jump Side Kick can be executed as a regular kick with the front leg, or spinning-style using the rear leg (as illustrated).

Step forward with the back leg, then jump off and kick with the other leg. Extend your kicking leg while tucking the other leg in.

JUMP INSIDE-TO-OUTSIDE KICK

- From a fighting stance, jump up with clockwise motion.
- While sighting target, perform an Inside-to-Outside Jump Kick with the trailing leg.

JUMP OUTSIDE-TO-INSIDE KICK

- From a fighting stance, jump up with counter clockwise motion.
- While sighting target, perform an Outside-to-Inside Jump Kick with the trailing leg.

JUMP SPINNING HOOK KICK

- After launching the kick, roll hips over like for the side kick and then hook.
- When performing the hook kick, keep your kicking path parallel to the floor.
- Strike the target with the heel of your foot.

Stepping Forward Jump Hook Kick

18. Basic Plyometrics

What is Plyometrics

Often times these powerful exercises are ignored due to their difficult physical and time requirements. But if they are used wisely along with regular training, overall martial arts skill will improve. Many people do not know what plyometrics is or they have a distorted understanding of it. It is done to improve speed and power in any of the techniques. To improve speed and power rapid eccentric contraction is needed. What is meant by rapid eccentric contraction? This is the rapid lengthening of the muscle led by the rapid shortening of the muscle called concentric contraction. Only when these two components are done, following each other, will maximum speed and power be achieved. It may also be thought as the rapid stretching of the muscle. If the length of stretch is maximized and the time needed to complete the stretch is minimized then maximal power will occur. These exercises can be done to improve kicks or punches and often times they are used to improve jumping ability. Plyometric theory can be applied to any of the techniques, as it is the improvement of explosive power that is the issue.

In this next section the basic exercises will be explained. Remember it is always important to properly warm up and stretch before attempting any of these exercises, otherwise no gains will be made and actually some ground may be lost.

Basic Exercises

Double Leg Bound 1
Jump forwards using both legs. Aim for both height and distance. Swing the arms up to produce momentum and a full body stretch. Land on both feet on the balls of the foot. Repeat immediately with 6-8 jumps. This should be done with intermittent resting for 3-5 sets.

Double Zigzag Leg Bound

Jump from side to side while advancing forward using both legs aiming for both height and distance. Keep the arms in a stationary position and bring the knees to the chest. When landing use the force of the landing to produce the springing energy needed for the next jump. Do 10 jumps for 3-5 sets being sure to rest in between in the same manner as stated above.

Double Leg Bound 2

Begin squatting with one leg behind the other. The hands should be pulled behind the back of the head. Jump aiming for height, alternate the position of the legs in mid-air. Do not release the arms while performing this exercise. Land and repeat immediately 6-8 jumps. Continue as stated before 3-5 sets with resting in between.

Knees to Chest

Jump upward using both legs aiming for height. Keep the arms in a stationary position and bring the knees to the chest. When landing use the force of the landing to produce the springing energy needed for the next jump. Do 10 jumps for 3-5 sets being sure to rest in between in the same manner as stated above.

Ballistic pushups

Begin in regular pushup position and in an explosive action, push the body up so that it is possible to clap the hands together. Repeat this 10 times and rest for a minute or two between sets. Complete 3-5 sets.

● Exercises with a Medicine Ball

A medicine ball is a heavy ball usually made of either solid polyurethane, gel or air. They are produced in different sizes, from light to heavier weight . They are used for all sorts of exercises.

Medicine Ball 1
These exercises are to be done with a partner and a Medicine Ball. Begin facing each other at a distance of about 5-6 feet apart. Using explosive speed and power push the ball toward your partner. Each partner repeats 10 throws and rests for 1-2 minutes. Repeat 3-5 sets.

Medicine Ball 2
Begin by facing the same direction standing about 5-6 feet apart. Without moving the feet turn the body to one side, throwing the ball toward your partner. Your partner should catch the ball by turning the body to the side without moving the orientation of the feet. Your partner should throw the ball back in the same way. Repeat this exercise with 10 throws repeat on alternate side 2-3 times with resting in between.

Medicine Ball 3
Begin by standing in a stable position and push the ball up with explosive action. Catch and repeat for 10 throws 2-3 sets with rest in between.

All these exercises are intended to be done with an extreme amount of effort, of course never push to the point of injury. With this in mind be sure to rest adequately between sets because the most will be achieved if the muscles have the opportunity to recover, and perform again at a maximum level. Other exercises may be incorporated into a plyometric workout. For instance the performing of regular techniques may be done with an emphasis on maximum power and stretch in a minimal amount of time.

19. Information on Each Hyung

Name of Hyung	Name of Creator	Date of Creation	Total # of movements*	Point of Kihap	Ideal Completion Time	Characteristic
KEE CHO HYUNG IL BU	Kwan Jang Nim Hwang Kee	1947	20	8, 16	30-35 sec	Baby's First Steps
KEE CHO HYUNG EE BU	Kwan Jang Nim Hwang Kee	1947	20	8, 16	30-35 sec	Baby's First Steps
KEE CHO HYUNG SAM BU	Kwan Jang Nim Hwang Kee	1947	20	8, 16	30-35 sec	Baby's First Steps
PYUNG AHN CHO DAN HYUNG	Mr. Idos	Approximately 1870	22	10, 18	30-35 sec	Turtle
PYUNG AHN EE DAN HYUNG	Mr. Idos	Approximately 1870	29	8, 12, 29	35-40 sec	Turtle
PYUNG AHN SAM DAN HYUNG	Mr. Idos	Approximately 1870	27	8, 10, 27	35-40 sec	Turtle
PYUNG AHN SA DAN HYUNG	Mr. Idos	Approximately 1870	27	12, 25	35-40 sec	Turtle
PYUNG AHN OH DAN HYUNG	Mr. Idos	Approximately 1870	28	11, 21	40-45 sec	Turtle
CHIL SUNG IL ROH HYUNG	Kwan Jang Nim Hwang Kee	In the 1980's	38	12, 30	65-70 sec	Seven Stars
CHIL SUNG EE ROH HYUNG	Kwan Jang Nim Hwang Kee	In the 1980's	29	14, 25	45-50 sec	Seven Stars
BASSAI	unknown	1550	52	21, 28, 52	60-65 sec	Snake
NAI HAN CHI CHO DAN	Jang Song Kae	Around 1070 'Song Dynasty'	27	14, 27	25 sec	Horse

*(excluding Joon Bee & Ba Ro Jaseh)

20. Forms, One Step Sparring, Self Defense, Free Sparring & Breaking

● Forms (Hyungs) 형

Forms, or *Hyungs*, are highly choreographed movements designed to link offensive and defensive techniques into set patterns. By performing hyungs, the student not only learns how to connect basic techniques, but also will improve on power, speed, timing, strength, flexibility, breath control and focus. All these attributes are essential when free sparring, or in a real life situation of self defense.

Hyungs are not unique to Tang Soo Do, but are traditional in many of the martial art styles. In Tang Soo Do, many of the hyungs are hundreds of years old, being passed down from master to master. Within them can be found characteristics of Okinawan Karate and Chinese *Kung Fu* (*Wu Shu*). In a sense, the hyungs represent the core of our art, linking the present with the past.

Later in this manual, hyungs practiced at the various belt levels (Gup) will be described in detail, including their origins and characteristics.

● One Step Sparring (Il Soo Sik Dae Ryun) 일수식 대련

One-step sparring is a traditional element of Tang Soo Do performed with a partner to practice defensive and offensive techniques without contact. Unlike the hyungs, one-steps are not passed down unchanged, but are created by each instructor, reflecting that person's creativity and use of techniques. Tang Soo Do Moo Duk Kwan has developed 18 one-steps that are learned by students as they progress through the Gup ranks. These one-steps become progressively more complex and demanding skill-wise, commensurate with rank. Later in this manual, various one-steps will be described in detail for each Gup level.

● Self Defense (Ho Sin Sool) 호신술

Like the one-steps, self defense techniques are developed by individual instructors based on what they have learned from their masters, and their own application of techniques. In this manual, self defense techniques are presented for when an attacker grabs one or both of your hands. In general, each technique is a series of moves designed to first break the attacker's grip, then to counter attack with offensive measures. As with hyungs and one-steps, different Gup levels require mastery of certain self defense techniques.

SPEED:
In Self-Defense and One-Step Sparring practice all techniques should be performed at maximum speed and power. It should take approximately *1 to 2 seconds* from your first technique (reaction) to the last and finishing move.

● Free Sparring (*Ja Yu Dae Ryun*) 자유 대련

Free Sparring is the ultimate representation of the art of Tang Soo Do. This is because free sparring is the closest demonstration of actual combat, which is the primary purpose Tang Soo Do is used to train for. All of the exercises *Ho Sin Sool, Il Soo Sik Dae Ryun* and *Hyungs* lead to the preparation of actual combat. Even those who claim not to be training for combat and wish only for the benefit of exercise, inadvertently train for combat. This is because the intentions of the motions are implied in the movement. These intentions are most easily seen when they are incorporated within the framework of free sparring. Even those who claim to be doing it for arts sake, not for the sake of combat, miss the point of Tang Soo Do. Tang Soo Do is a complete martial art, which incorporates all aspects of martial art training, artistic or not. For those who train only for the art they are not complete martial artists.

With the understanding of free sparring as the ultimate expression of Tang Soo Do, comes the understanding that the practice of sparring entails a great deal of respect for the demonstration of the art. The demonstration includes bowing to both instructor and partner before and after the demonstration, it includes bowing or showing some indication of respect when a point has been landed.

Respect is also demonstrated by not using full force. This respect is given to the power of the technique, as well as the partner with whom one is training. By not using full force while sparring the full power of the technique is given consideration. It is understood that the full force of techniques can be crippling or even deadly. That is why sparring is done with little or no contact. It is referred as control of power, the sixth of the "Ten Key Concepts", *Him Cho Chung*. This respect extends to ones partner. When sparring in class, ones partner is given full respect, because they allow the practice of the art. It is also the partners opportunity to benefit from the training. In this respect both participants in free sparring should treat each other as partners, training for the benefit of the other.

Sparring Quick Points:

-Sparring is not about power, but about speed and timing.
-Test your opponent (ie. Fake attacks, set up motions).
-Combinations: multiple attacks are better than single attacks.
-Use motions that flow from each other.
-When evading try to move laterally,side to side, try not to move backwards.
-Develop techniques from multiple angles- even when falling.

● Breaking (*Kyok Pa*) 격파

Board breaking using different kicks and hand strikes traditionally is done during promotional testing. Breaking demonstrates correct application of technique, power and focus. A person can have great power, but if he or she lacks focus or technique, will not break. As one progresses through the Gups, breaking requirements become more challenging.

When holding the board, make sure fingers are flat and arms are locked in place.

YELLOW BELT

GENERAL REQUIREMENTS

1. These ranks are assigned to individuals of good moral character who have been accepted as students by an officially recognized Dan member of the Hwa Rang World Tang Soo Do Moo Duk Kwan Federation.
2. No age requirement, but must be a member of the Hwa Rang World Tang Soo Do Moo Duk Kwan Federation in good standing.
3. Regular weekly Studio attendance.

Kee Cho Il Bu
Page 80

GENERAL KNOWLEDGE

1. Conceptual knowledge of basic technique.
2. General rules of class conduct.
3. Basic Tang Soo Do etiquette.
4. Elementary Tang Soo Do terminology.

DEMONSTRATION OF ABILITY

1. BASIC MOVEMENT (KEE CHO):
  Hand techniques: low block, high block, inside block, outside block, middle punch, high punch, and side punch.
  Foot techniques: front stretch kick, inside-outside kick, outside-inside kick, front snap kick, front thrust kick, roundhouse kick, and jump front thrust kick.

One Step Sparring
Page 84

2. FORMS (HYUNG):
  Kee Cho Hyung Il Bu

3. ONE STEP SPARRING (IL SOO SIK DAE RYUN): #1 & 2

4. SELF DEFENSE (HO SIN SOOL):
Cross-hand Grip #1 & 2, Studio #1 & 2

Self Defense
Page 85

5. BREAKING (KYOK PA): Elbow or Front Thrust Kick
  (Children under 10 will break a half-sized board.)

6. TERMINOLOGY:

Breaking
Page 90

Name of the art you are taking	Tang Soo Do
Name of organization	Hwa Rang World Tang Soo Do Moo Duk Kwan Federation
Name of Instructor	Full Name
Uniform	도복 *Do Bok*
Studio	도장 *Do Jang*
Seniors	선배 *Sun Beh*
Juniors	후배 *Hu Beh*

기
초
형

일
부

2. Kee Cho Hyung Il Bu
Basic Form 1 (20 movements)

RIGHT 1st LINE   BACK   LEFT 1st LINE

RIGHT   CENTER LINE   LEFT

RIGHT 2nd LINE   FRONT   LEFT 2nd LINE

A thousand-mile journey starts with the first step. This form is like a baby's first step. It is the one that must be understood in order to go on to the next. Tang Soo Do is impressive for its many techniques. The *Kee Cho* forms are the basis for all movements that follow it.

    The *Kee Cho, Pyung Ahn*, and some of the *Chil Sung hyung*'s go in the direction of a capitol "I" or "H". When turning to perform each move it is necessary to turn to the middle part of the "I", as shown in the following illustration.

❶ *Ha Dan Mahk Kee*
(*Shi Sun:* Look to the left). Turn to the left 90° with a defensive hip turn and perform a *Ha Dan Mahk Kee* (down block) with the left hand.

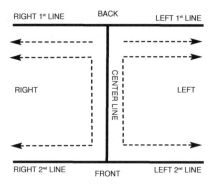

Joon Bee is not a technique, it is a stance. In this position one's mind should be empty waiting for a command.

❷ *Jung Dan Kong Kyuk*
Step forward with the right foot using an offensive hip turn and perform a *Jung Dan Kong Kyuk* (middle punch) with the right hand. Your first two knuckles should be at your solar plexus's height when performing a middle punch.

Solar Plexus height

❸ *Ha Dan Mahk Kee*
(*Shi Sun*: Look over the right shoulder to the rear). Stepping back with the right leg turn to your right 180° and perform a *Ha Dan Mahk Kee* with the right hand.

❹ Jung Dan Kong Kyuk
Step forward with the left foot using an offensive hip turn and perform a *Jung Dan Kong Kyuk* (middle punch) with the left fist.

❺ Ha Dan Mahk Kee
(*Shi Sun*: Look to the left). Turn to the left 90° stepping with the left leg into the center line of the form, and perform a *Ha Dan Mahk Kee* (down block) with the left hand.

❻ Jung Dan Kong Kyuk
Step forward with the right leg using an offensive hip and perform a *Jung Dan Kong Kyuk* (middle punch) with the right fist.

❼ Jung Dan Kong Kyuk
Step forward with the left leg using an offensive hip and perform a *Jung Dan Kong Kyuk* with the left fist.

❽ Jung Dan Kong Kyuk
Step forward with the right leg using an offensive hip; perform a *Jung Dan Kong Kyuk* with the right fist and simultaneously *Ki Hap* (yell).

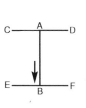

❾ Ha Dan Mahk Kee
Look over the left shoulder to the rear stepping with the left leg. Turn 270° to the left and perform a *Ha Dan Mahk Kee* with the left hand.

⑩ *Jung Dan Kong Kyuk*
Step forward with the right leg using an offensive hip and perform a *Jung Dan Kong Kyuk* with the right fist.

⑪ *Ha Dan Mahk Kee*
(*Shi Sun*: Look over the right shoulder). Stepping with the right leg turn 180° to the right and perform a *Ha Dan Mahk Kee* with the right hand.

⑫ *Jung Dan Kong Kyuk*
Step forward with the left foot using an offensive hip and perform a *Jung Dan Kong Kyuk* with the left fist.

⑬ *Ha Dan Mahk Kee*
(*Shi Sun*: Look to the left). Stepping out with the left foot turn 90° to the left and perform a *Ha Dan Mahk Kee* with the left hand.

⑭ *Jung Dan Kong Kyuk*
Step forward with the right leg using an offensive hip and perform a *Jung Dan Kong Kyuk* with the right fist.

⑮ *Jung Dan Kong Kyuk*
Step forward with the left foot using an offensive hip and perform a *Jung Dan Kong Kyuk* with the left fist.

16 *Jung Dan Kong Kyuk*
Step forward with the right leg using an offensive hip, perform a *Jung Dan Kong Kyuk* with the right hand and simultaneously *Ki Hap*.

17 *Ha Dan Mahk Kee*
Look over the left shoulder. Stepping with the left leg turn 270° to the left and perform a *Ha Dan Mahk Kee* with the left hand.

18 *Jung Dan Kong Kyuk*
Step forward with the right leg using an offensive hip turn and perform a *Jung Dan Kong Kyuk* with the right fist.

19 *Ha Dan Mahk Kee*
Look over the right shoulder. Stepping with the right foot turn 180° to the right and perform a *Ha Dan Mahk Kee* with the right hand.

20 *Jung Dang Kong Kyuk*
Step forward with the left leg using an offensive hip and perform a *Jung Dan Kon Kyuk* with the left fist.

Ba Ro
Bring left foot back to return to *Ba Ro Jaseh*.

Applications for Kee Cho Hyung Il Bu

- Down Block and Middle Punch

Ha Dan Mahk Kee

Jung Dan Kong Kyuk

The **Ki Hap** (or **Kiai** in Japanese) is the sound that results from explosive release of internal energy. The Japanese word **Ki** ("*Qi* or *Chi*" in Chinese) translates as "life force" or "internal energy". *Ai* means "to blend" or "concentrate". The *Ki Hap* then means to "concentrate one's life force of energy". It comes from the expelling of air from the abdomen (not the throat), and it sounds like a strong 'yell', but can also be silent. During One-Step Sparring for example, it helps you gather your energy and focus; coordinate your actions; and is a motivator for the martial arts practitioner.

---

3. One Step Sparring (*Il Soo Sik Dae Ryun*)
일수식 대련

- Number 1

Both participants begin by bowing and finding a proper distance at which to perform the techniques. This can be done by having the participants raise fists so that they meet. Next, the attacking member will simultaneously step back with the right foot into a front stance; perform a low block with the left hand and *Ki Hap*. The senior member will remain in *Joon Bee Jaseh* in preparation for the rest of the exercise. The defending member will *Ki Hap*, signaling to the attacker that they are ready.

The attacker steps forward with the right foot and performs a *Jung Dan Kong Kyuk* to the base of the defender's nose.

❶ In response the defender steps with the right foot to the right corner at a 45° angle and performs an *Ahneso Pakuro Soo Do Mahk Kee* with the left hand, blocking the punch.

❷ The defender then twists the body 90° to the left performing a *Jung Dan Kong Kyuk* with the right fist. This punch is directed at the solar plexus of the attacker.

❸ Next the defender turns the hip over 90° to the right and performs a *Sang Dan Kong Kyuk* with the left fist to the base of the nose.

❹ The defender will then pull the left foot back behind the right foot in preparation for the next motion. In this position the hands are raised in defense and the knees are bent slightly.

❺ Next the defending member performs a roundhouse kick to the side of the attacker's head with the right foot. *Ki Hap*.

❻ Immediatley the defender brings the right leg back behind the left leg coming to fighting stance.

In closing, both members simultaneously return to *Ba Ro Jaseh* and bow. ■

• Number 2

The defending member will *Ki Hap*, signaling to the attacker that they are ready.

❶ The attacker steps forward with the right foot and performs a *Jung Dan Kong Kyuk* to the base of the defender's nose. In response the defender steps with the left foot to the left corner at a 45° angle and performs an *Ahneso Pakuro Soo Do Mahk Kee* with the right hand, blocking the punch.

❷ The defender then twists the body 90° to the right performing a *Jung Dan Kong Kyuk* with the left fist. This punch is directed at the solar plexus of the attacker.

❸ Next the defender turns the hip over 90° to the left and perform a *Sang Dan Kong Kyuk* with the right fist to the base of the nose.

❹The defender then pulls the right foot back behind the left foot in preparation for the next motion. In this position the hands are raised in defense and the knees are bent slightly.

❺Next the defending member performs a roundhouse kick to the side of the attacker's head with the left foot. *Ki Hap*.

❻Immediatley the defending member brings the left leg back behind the right leg coming to fighting stance.

In closing, both members simultaneously return to *Ba Ro Jaseh* and bow. ▪

4. Self Defense (*Ho Sin Sool*)
호신술

- Cross Hand #1

Both participants begin by bowing and finding a proper distance at which to perform the exercise. The attacker proceeds by using the right hand to grab the defender's right wrist.

❶The defender steps to the right corner at a 45°, then turning the hip to the left 90°, moving the right arm over the attacker's right arm to break the hold.

❷Immediately the defender snaps the hip to the left, using the right hand to perform a high knife-hand strike to the attacker's neck.

❸The defender then twists the hip 90° to the right and uses the left hand to perform a high palm strike to the base of the attacker's nose.

❹The defender then twists the hip 90° to the left into *Jun Gul Jaseh* and uses the right hand to perform a spear hand attack to the attacker's groin. This technique is done with a *Ki Hap*.

In closing, both members bow and return to *Ba Ro Jaseh*. ∎

• Cross Hand #2

Both participants begin by bowing and finding a proper distance at which to complete the exercise. The defender proceeds by using the right hand to grab the defender's right wrist.

❶The defender raises the left hand so that it is just over the right shoulder.
❷Immediately the defender steps with the right leg to the right corner at a 45° into *Jun Gul Jaseh,* using the left hand to perform a high knife-hand strike to the attacker's neck. The defender's right hand is raised just behind the head.

❸The defender immediately twists the hip 90° to the left, using the right hand to perform a high palm strike to the base of the attacker's nose.

❹The defender then twists the hip 90° to the right into *Jun Gul Jaseh,* using the left hand to perform a spear-hand strike to the attacker's groin. This technique is done with a *Ki Hap.*

In closing, both members bow and return to *Ba Ro Jaseh.* ■

5. Breaking (*Kyo Pa*)
격파

• Elbow Strike

- Focus your power on the center of the board.
- Use your hip motion to drive the front face of your elbow through the board.

• Front Thrust Kick

- Kick with the ball of the foot.
- Thrust through the board using your hips.

ORANGE BELT

GENERAL REQUIREMENTS
1. Sound moral character.
2. No age requirement, but must be a member of the Hwa Rang World Tang Soo Do Moo Duk Kwan Federation, in good standing.
3. Regular weekly Studio attendance.

GENERAL KNOWLEDGE
1. Conceptual knowledge of basic technique.
2. General rules of class conduct.
3. Basic Tang Soo Do etiquette.
4. Elementary Tang Soo Do terminology.

DEMONSTRATION OF ABILITY
1. **BASIC MOVEMENT (KEE CHO):**
   Hand techniques: low block, high block, inside block, outside block, middle punch, high punch, side punch, and Hu Gul Jaseh Ahneso Phakuro Mahk Kee.
   Foot techniques: front stretch kick, inside-outside kick, outside-inside kick, front snap kick, front thrust kick, roundhouse kick, side kick, spinning back kick, and jump front thrust kick.

2. **FORMS (HYUNG):**
   Kee Cho Hyung Il Bu, Kee Cho Hyung Ee Bu, Kee Cho Hyung Sam Bu, Hwa Rang Tournament Form #1 (recommended)

3. **ONE STEP SPARRING (IL SOO SIK DAE RYUN):** #1 - 4

4. **SELF DEFENSE (HO SIN SOOL):**
   Cross-hand Grip #1 - 4, Studio #1 & 2

5. **BREAKING (KYOK PA):** Hammer Punch or Knife Hand
   (Children under 10 will break a half-sized board.)

6. **TERMINOLOGY:**

Name of the art you are taking.....	Tang Soo Do
Name of organization...........................	Hwa Rang World Tang Soo Do Moo Duk Kwan Federation
Name of Instructor................................	Full Name
Instructor..	사범님 *Sa Bom Nim* (4th Dan and up; Licensed Instructor)
Uniform...	도복 *Do Bok*
Studio...	도장 *Do Jang*
Courage...	용기 *Yong Gi*
Junior...	후배 *Hu Beh*
Seniors...	선배 *Sun Beh*

Kee Cho Ee Bu
Page 92

Kee Cho Sam Bu
Page 96

One Step Sparring
Page 101

Self Defense
Page 103

Breaking
Page 106

기초형 이부

2. Kee Cho Hyung Ee Bu
Basic Form 2 (20 movements)

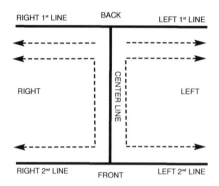

RIGHT 1ˢᵗ LINE   BACK   LEFT 1ˢᵗ LINE

RIGHT   CENTER LINE   LEFT

RIGHT 2ⁿᵈ LINE   FRONT   LEFT 2ⁿᵈ LINE

The second of the basic forms follows the same pattern as the first with a few changes in technique. These changes include the addition of the high block and high punch. When executing a high punch it is important to remember where your target is. The target for a high punch is the *In Jung* (base of the nose). The second change is in the high block. With this technique as with all blocks one must block with the bone and not the inside of the arm.

Begin in *Joon Bee Jaseh*, feet parallel and hands one fist apart.

❶ *Ha Dan Mahk Kee*
Turn 90° to the left and execute a *Ha Dan Mahk Kee* with the left hand.

❷ *Sang Dan Kong Kyuk*
Step forward with the left leg using an offensive hip turn and execute a *Sang Dan Kong Kyuk* (high punch) with the right fist.

base of nose = fist height

back leg straight

❸ *Ha Dan Mahk Kee*
Stepping back with the right leg turn 180° to the right and execute a *Ha Dan Mahk Kee* with the the right hand.

❹ *Sang Dan Kong Kyuk*
Step forward with the right leg using an offensive hip turn and execute a *Sang Dan Kong Kyuk* with the left fist. The High punch's target is the base of the nose.

❺ *Ha Dan Mahk Kee*
Stepping with the left leg turn 90° to the left and execute a *Ha Dan Mahk Kee* with the left hand.

❻ *Sang Dan Mahk Kee*
Step forward with the right leg using a defensive hip and execute a *Sang Dan Mahk Kee* (high block) with the right hand.

❼ *Sang Dan Mahk Kee*
Step forward with the left leg using a defensive hip and execute a *Sang Dan Mahk Kee* with the left hand.

❽ *Sang Dan Mahk Kee*
Step forward with the right leg using a defensive hip; execute a *Sang Dan Mahk Kee* with the right hand and simultaneously *Ki Hap*.

❾ *Ha Dan Mahk Kee*
Stepping with the left leg turn 270° and execute a *Ha Dan Mahk Kee* with the left hand.

❿ Sang Dan Kong Kyuk
Step forward with the right foot using an offensive hip and perform a *Sang Dan Kong Kyuk* with the right fist.

⓫ Ha Dan Mahk Kee
Step with the right leg and turn 180° to the right performing a *Ha Dan Mahk Kee* with the right hand.

⓬ Sang Dan Kong Kyuk
Step forward with the left leg using an offensive hip and perform a *Sang Dan Kong Kyuk* with the left fist.

⓭ Ha Dan Mahk Kee
Step with the left leg and turn 90° to the left performing a *Ha Dan Mahk Kee* with the left hand.

⓮ Sang Dan Mahk Kee
Step forward with the right leg using a defensive hip and perform a *Sang Dan Kong Kyuk* with the right hand.

⓯ Sang Dan Mahk Kee
Step forward with the left leg using a defensive hip and perform a *Sang Dan Mahk Kee* with the left hand.

16 *Sang Dan Mahk Kee*
Step forward with the right leg using a defensive hip, perform a *Sang Dan Mahk Kee* with the right hand and simultaneously *Ki Hap*.

17 *Ha Dan Mahk Kee*
Step back with the left leg and turn 270° to the left and perform a *Ha Dan Mahk Kee* with the left hand.

18 *Sang Dan Kong Kyuk*
Step forward with the right leg using an offensive hip and perform a *Sang Dan Kong Kyuk* with the right fist.

19 *Ha Dan Mahk Kee*
Step back with the right leg and turn 180° to the right performing a *Ha Dan Mahk Kee* with the right hand.

20 *Sang Dang Kong Kyuk*
Step forward with the left leg using an offensive hip and perform a *Sang Dan Kong Kyuk* with the left fist.

Ba Ro
Bring left foot back and return to *Ba Ro Jaseh*.

기
초
형
삼
부

2. Kee Cho Hyung Sam Bu
Basic Form 3 (20 movements)

RIGHT 1ˢᵗ LINE — BACK — LEFT 1ˢᵗ LINE

RIGHT — CENTER LINE — LEFT

RIGHT 2ⁿᵈ LINE — FRONT — LEFT 2ⁿᵈ LINE

The third of the *Kee Cho* forms is altered only slightly from the first and the second. It keeps the same basic "I" shape but it includes two new stances and one new block. These are *Hu Gul Jaseh* and *Kee Mah Jaseh*. *Hu Gul Jaseh*, also called "back stance", places 75% of one's weight on the back foot, and 25% on the front. The front leg should only have the ball of the foot touching. This form may be difficult for beginners not accustomed to switching into different stances. While moving from position to position it is important to keep your head at the same level.

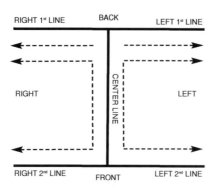

Begin in *Joon Bee Jaseh*, feet parallel and hands one fist apart.

one fist apart

C —— A —— D
E —— B —— F

❶ *Hu Gul Jaseh Ahneso Pakuro Mahk Kee*
(*Shi Sun*: Look to the left). Turn 90° to the left and execute a *Hu Gul Jaseh Ahneso Pakuro Mahk Kee* with the left hand.

C —— A →— D
E —— B —— F

❷ *Jung Dan Kong Kyuk*
Step forward with an offensive hip turn and execute a *Jung Dan Kong Kyuk* with the right fist.

C —— A →— D
E —— B —— F

❸ *Hu Gul Jaseh Ahneso Pakuro Mahk Kee*
(*Shi Sun*: Look over the right shoulder to the rear). Turn 180° to the right executing a *Hu Gul Jaseh Ahneso Pakuro Mahk Kee* with the right hand.

base of nose

C —← A —— D
E —— B —— F

4 *Jung Dan Kong Kyuk*
Step forward with the left leg using an offensive hip turn and execute a *Jung Dan Kong Kyuk* with the left fist.

5 *Ha Dan Mahk Kee*
(*Shi Sun*: Look to the left). Step with the left right leg and turn 90° to the left executing *a Ha Dan Mahk Kee* with the left hand.

6 *Wheng Jin Kong Kyuk*
Step forward with the right leg using an offensive hip turn and execute a *Wheng Jin Kong Kyuk* (side punch) with the right fist.

7 *Wheng Jin Kong Kyuk*
Step forward with the left leg using an offensive hip turn and execute a *Wheng Jin Kong Kyuk* with the left hand.

8 *Wheng Jin Kong Kyuk*
Step forward with the right leg using an offensive hip; execute a *Wheng Jin Kong Kyuk* with the right fist and simultaneously *Ki Hap*.

9 *Hu Gul Jaseh Ahneso Pakuro Mahk Kee*
Look over the left shoulder to the rear. Step back with the left leg and turn 270° to the left executing a *Hu Gul Jaseh Ahneso Pakuro Mahk Kee* with the left hand.

❿ *Jung Dan Kong Kyuk*
Step forward with an offensive hip and perform a *Jung Dan Kong Kyuk* with the right hand.

⓫ *Hu Gul Jaseh Ahneso Pakuro Mahk Kee*
Look over the right shoulder to the rear. Turn 180° to the right and perform a *Hu Gul Jaseh Ahneso Pakuro Mahk Kee* with the right hand.

⓬ *Jung Dan Kong Kyuk*
Step forward with an offensive hip and perform a *Jung Dan Kong Kyuk* with the left hand.

⓭ *Ha Dan Mahk Kee*
Look to the left. Turn 90° to the left and perform a *Ha Dan Mahk Kee* with the left hand.

⓮ *Wheng Jin Kong Kyuk*
Step forward with an offensive hip and perform a *Wheng Jin Kong Kyuk* with the right hand.

⓯ *Wheng Jin Kong Kyuk*
Step forward with an offensive hip and perform a *Wheng Jin Kong Kyuk* with the left hand.

16 *Wheng Jin Kong Kyuk*
Step forward with a offensive hip; perform a *Wheng Jin kong Kyuk* with the right hand and simultaneously *Ki Hap*.

17 *Hu Gul Jaseh Ahneso Pakuro Mahk Kee*
Look over the left shoulder to the rear. Turn 270° to the left and perform a *Hu Gul Jaseh Ahneso Pakuro Mahk Kee*.

18 *Jung Dan Kong Kyuk*
Step forward with an offensive hip and perform a *Jung Dan Kong Kyuk* with the right fist.

19 *Hu Gul Jaseh Ahneso Pakuro Mahk Kee*
Look over the right shoulder to the rear. Turn 180° to the right and perform a *Hu Gul Jaseh Ahneso Pakuro Mahk Kee*.

20 *Jung Dan Kong Kyuk*
Step forward with an offensive hip and perform a *Jung Dan Kong Kyuk*.

Ba Ro
Bring left foot back to return *Ba Ro Jaseh*.

Applications for Kee Cho Hyung Ee Bu & Sam Bu

• Down Block, High Punch and High Block

Ha Dan Mahk Kee *Sang Dan Kong Kyuk* *Sang Dan Mahk Kee*

• Inside Outside Block and Side Punch

Ahneso Pakuro Mahk Kee *Wheng Jin Kong Kyuk*

3. One Step Sparring (*Il Soo Sik Dae Ryun*)
일수식 대련

• Number 3

❶The defending member will *Ki Hap*, signaling to the attacker that they are ready. The attacker steps forward with the right foot and performs a *Jung Dan Kong Kyuk* with the right fist. In response the defender steps with the right foot to the right corner at a 45° angle and performs a *Pakeso Ahnuro Mahk Kee* with the right hand, blocking the punch.

❷The defender will then twist the body 180° to the right and perform *Jung Dan Kong Kyuk* with the right left. This punch is directed at the solar plexus of the attacker.

❸Next the defender will turn the hip 180° to the left, performing a *Sang Dan Kong Kyuk* with the right fist to the base of the nose.

❹The defender will then pull the left foot back behind the right foot in preparation for the next motion. In this position the hands are raised in defense and the knees are bent slightly.

❺Next the defending member will perform a side-kick with the right foot to the solar-plexus of the attacker and simultaneously *Ki Hap* .

❻Immediatley the defending member will bring the right leg back behind the left leg and come to fighting stance.

In closing, both members simultaneously return to *Baro Jaseh* and bow. ■

• Number 4

❶The defending member will *Ki Hap*, signaling to the attacker that they are ready. The attacker steps forward with the right foot and performs a *Jung Dan Kong Kyuk*. In response the defender steps with the left foot to the left corner at a 45° angle and performs a *Pakeso Ahnuro Mahk Kee* with the left hand, blocking the punch.

❷The defender will then twist the body 180° to the left, performing a *Jung Dan Kong Kyuk* with the right fist to the ribs.

❸Next the defender will turn the hip over 180° to the right and perform a *Sang Dan Kong Kyuk* with the left fist to the base of the nose.

❹The defender will then pull the right foot back behind the left foot in preparation for the next motion. In this position the hands are raised in defense and the knees are bent slightly.

❺Next the defending member will perform a side-kick with the left foot to the solar plexus or head of the attacker and simultaneously *Ki Hap*. Immediately the defending member will bring the left leg back behind the right leg and come to fighting stance.

In closing, both members simultaneously return to *Ba Ro Jaseh* and bow.■

4. Self Defense (*Ho Sin Sool*)
호신술

- Cross Hand #3

  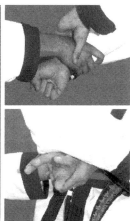

Both participants begin by bowing and finding a proper distance at which to complete the exercise. The defender proceeds by using the right hand to grab the defender's right wrist.

❶The defender lifts up the right hand so that the palm is facing the attacker. With the left hand, grab the attackers right wrist, so that the thumb is placed on the back of the hand.

Back View

Back View

❷While keeping a firm grip on the attacker's wrist, the defender steps with the right leg to left corner at a 45° into *Sa Ko Rip Jaseh*. By doing this, the attacker's right arm is turned over on itself, disabling the attacker.

❸In the same stance the defender performs an elbow strike with the right arm to the attacker's head. This is done while the left hand is keeping a firm grip on the attacker's wrist.

❹Immediately the defender trades hands, using the right hand to hold onto the attacker's wrist. The defender then turns to the left into back-stance, using the left arm to perform a spinning back elbow strike to the attacker's solar plexus. This final technique is done with a *Ki Hap*.

In closing, both members bow and return to *Ba Ro Jaseh*. ■

• Cross Hand #4

Both participants begin by bowing and finding a proper distance at which to complete the exercise. The defender proceeds by using the right hand to grab the defender's right wrist.

❶ The defender uses the right hand, holding onto the attacker's right wrist and the left hand to hold onto the back of the attacker's wrist.

❷ While keeping a firm grip on the attacker's wrist, the defender immediately steps with the left leg to the right corner at a 45° into front-stance. With this movement the attacker's grip is effectively broken.

❸ While keeping a firm grip on the attacker's wrist, the defender turns to the right, pivoting on the right foot and moving under the attacker's wrist. The defender continue pivoting until he/she is again facing the attacker.

❹ The defender pulls the attacker's arm down, locking the joint to cause "pain compliance".

❺ Finally the defender performs a head butt to the attacker's face and simultaneously *Ki Haps*.

In closing, both members bow and return to *Ba Ro Jaseh*. ▪

5. Breaking (*Kyo Pa*)
격파

• Hammer Punch

▪ As with the elbow strike, focus your attention on the center of the board.
▪ Use the bottom of your fist to strike the board.
▪ Use your body weight and hip rotation for power.

• Knife Hand

▪ As with the hammer strike, focus your attention on the center of the board.
▪ Use the edge of the hand to drive through the board.
▪ Use your body weight and hip rotation for power.

ORANGE BELT
WITH STRIPE

GENERAL REQUIREMENTS
1. Sound moral character.
2. No age requirement, but must be a member of the Hwa Rang World Tang Soo Do Moo Duk Kwan Federation, in good standing.
3. Regular weekly Studio attendance.

GENERAL KNOWLEDGE
1. Conceptual knowledge of lower rank techniques.
2. Understanding of Moo Duk Kwan spirit by demonstrated attitude.
3. Additional knowledge of the basic techniques of Tang Soo Do.

Pyung Ahn Cho Dan
Page 108

DEMONSTRATION OF ABILITY

1. **BASIC MOVEMENT (KEE CHO):**
   Hand techniques: Soo Do low block, reverse punches (high and middle), low block
   Foot techniques: front thrust and inside-outside kick combination, roundhouse kick, side kick, jump front kick, jump inside-outside kick, and jump outside-inside kick.

One Step Sparring
Page 114

2. **FORMS (HYUNG):**
   Kee Cho Hyung Sam Bu, Pyung Ahn Cho Dan, Hwa Rang Tournament Form #1

3. **ONE STEP SPARRING (IL SOO SIK DAE RYUN):** #3 - 6

Self Defense
Page 116

4. **SELF DEFENSE (HO SIN SOOL):**
   Cross-hand #1 - 4, Straight hand #1 & 2, Studio #1 - 4

5. **BREAKING (KYOK PA):** Stepping behind sidekick.
   (Children under 10 will break a half-sized board.)

6. **TERMINOLOGY:**

Breaking
Page 118

Name of the art you are taking	Tang Soo Do
Name of organization	Hwa Rang World Tang Soo Do Moo Duk Kwan Federation
Name of Instructor	Full Name
Instructor	사범님 *Sa Bom Nim*
Seniors	선배님 *Sun Beh Nim*
Juniors	후배 *Hu Beh*
Uniform	도복 *Do Bok*
Studio	도장 *Do Jang*
Yong ki	용기 Courage
Chung Shin Tong Il	정신통일 Concentration
Counting (In Korean)	

평안 초단

2. Pyung Ahn Cho Dan Hyung
Pyung Ahn 1 (22 movements)

The Pyung forms were originally constructed over 130 years ago. Before they became the *Pyung Ahn* forms, they were all part of a single form called *Je Nam Hyung*. It's division into five parts later resulted in the introduction of the *Pyung Ahn* forms. Translated, *Pyung Ahn* means "peace of mind" and the animal characteristic is the turtle. Many people laugh at this explanation of the *Hyung*. The turtle is not seen as a good fighter. It seems more logical to have a dragon or a tiger as a form. But a turtle is also logical. The shell of a turtle is a wonderful defense system into which the turtle can withdraw at any time. They live very long lives, some over 100 years. When they travel they are in no hurry "slow and steady wins the race" or so it is said in "The Tortoise and the Hare". This ties into the "peace of mind" aspect of the form. A turtle has peace of mind therefore it takes it's time. This is a cornerstone of Tang Soo Do. While training it is important to be patient with oneself and take time to perfect technique. This is the only way to achieve the harmonization of the mind and body.

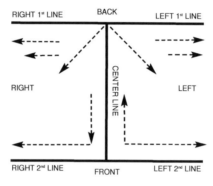

RIGHT 1ˢᵗ LINE — BACK — LEFT 1ˢᵗ LINE
RIGHT — CENTER LINE — LEFT
RIGHT 2ⁿᵈ LINE — FRONT — LEFT 2ⁿᵈ LINE

Joon Bee Jaseh
Ready stance facing north

❶ *Ha Dan Mahk Kee*
(*Shi Sun*: Look to the left). Step out with the left foot and perform a *Ha Dan Mahk Kee*.

❷ *Jung Dan Kong Kyuk*

Step forward with the right leg using an offensive hip turn and perform a *Jung Dan Kong Kyuk*.

❸ *Ha Dan Mahk Kee*

(*Shi Sun*: Look over the right shoulder to the rear). Turn 180° to the right. Step back with the right leg turning on the left and perform a *Ha Dan Mahk Kee* with the right hand.

front stance

❹ *Cap Kwon Kong Kyuk* (Back Fist)

A. While still in *Jun Gul Jaseh* bring the right arm in close to the body and the left arm over it so that they cross the chest. Then perform a *Cap Kwon Kong Kyuk* while simultaneously switching stances to *Sa Ko Rip Jaseh*. This motion can be either offensive or defensive since it's an effective escape from a wrist grab.

Kwon Do Kong Kyuk (Hammer strike)

B. Make a grabbing motion with the right hand and pull the arm in close to the body while dragging the right leg towards the left leg with both heels touching forming an 'L' shape. The position should be standing straight up. Perform a *Kwon Do Kong Kyuk* with the right hand.

Back fist
side stance

Hammer fist

❺ *Jung Dan Kong Kyuk*

Step forward with the left leg using an offensive hip turn and perform a *Jung Dan Kon Kyuk* with the left hand.

❻ *Ha Dan Mahk Kee*

(*Shi Sun:* Look to the left). Turn 90° to the left. Step out with the left foot and turn on the right to peform a *Ha Dan Mahk Kee*.

❼ Jung Dan Soo Do Mahk Kee
With a snap of the hip perform a *Jung Dan Soo Do Mahk Kee Kyuk* (middle knife hand block) with the right hand.

left!

❽ Sang Dan Mahk Kee
Step forward with the right leg using a defensive hip turn and perform a *Sang Dan Mahk Kee*.

❾ Sang Dan Mahk Kee
Step forward with the left leg using a defensive hip turn and perform a *Sang Dan Mahk Kee*.

❿ Sang Dan Mahk Kee
Step forward with the right leg using a defensive hip turn; perform a *Sang Dan Mahk Kee* and simultaneously *Ki Hap*.

⓫ Ha Dan Mahk Kee
(*Shi Sun*: Look over the left shoulder to the rear). Turn 270° to the left. Stepping out with the left foot and turning on the right peform a *Ha Dan Mahk Kee*.

⓬ Jung Dan Kong Kyuk
Step forward with the right leg using an offensive hip turn; perform a *Jung Dan Kong Kyuk* with the right hand.

13 *Ha Dan Mahk Kee*
(*Shi Sun:* Look over the right shoulder to the rear). Turn 180° to the right Step back with the right leg turning on the left and perform a *Ha Dan Mahk Kee* with the right hand.

14 **Jung Dan Kong Kyuk**
Step forward with the left leg using an offensive hip turn and perform a *Jung Dan Kong Kyuk*.

15 *Ha Dan Mahk Kee*
(*Shi Sun*: Look to left). Turn 90° to the left stepping out with the left leg while turning on the right; perform a *Ha Dan Mahk Kee* with the left hand.

16 *Jung Dan Kong Kyuk*
Step forward with the right leg using an offensive hip turn and perform a *Jung Dan Kong Kyuk* with the right hand.

17 *Jung Dan Kong Kyuk*
Step forward with the left leg using an offensive hip turn and perform a *Jung Dan Kong Kyuk* with the left hand.

18 *Jung Dan Kong Kyuk*
Step forward with the right leg using an offensive hip turn; perform a *Jung Dan Kong Kyuk* with the right hand and simultaneously *Ki Hap*.

⑲ Hu Gul Ha Dan Soo Do Mahk Kee

(*Shi Sun*: Look over the left shoulder to the rear). Turn 270° to the left. Stepping out with the left foot and turning on the right peform a *Hu Gul Ha Dan Soo Do Mahk Kee* (middle double knife hand block in back stance) with the left hand.

⑳ Hu Gul Ha Dan Soo Do Mahk Kee

(*Shi Sun*: Look to the right). Turn 45° to the right. Stepping out with the right foot and turning on the left peform a *Hu Gul Ha Dan Soo Do Mahk Kee* with the right hand.

㉑ Hu Gul Ha Dan Soo Do Mahk Kee

(*Shi Sun*: Look over the right shoulder to the rear). Turn 135° to the right. Stepping out with the right foot and turning on the left peform a *Hu Gul Ha Dan Soo Do Mahk Kee* with the right hand.

㉒ Hu Gul Ha Dan Soo Do Mahk Kee

(*Shi Sun*: Look to the left). Turn 45° to the left. Stepping out with the left foot and turning on the right peform a *Hu Gul Ha Dan Soo Do Mahk Kee* with the left hand.

Ba Ro

Bring the left leg in and return to *Ba Ro Jaseh*.

Applications for Pyung Ahn Cho Dan

Ha Dan Mahk Kee   *Soo Do Jung Dan Kong Kyuk*

Applications for techniques number 3,4 and 5

Hu Gul Soo Do Ha Dan Mahk Kee

3. One Step Sparring (*Il Soo Sik Dae Ryun*)
일수식 대련

Beginning with *Oh Bon* (#5) and *Yuk Bon* (#6) and continuing throughout the rest of the one-steps, each member will switch sides. This means that for all of the odd number one-steps, the attacker will attack with from the right side and the defender will defend from the right side as well. For the even number one-steps, only the left side will be used.

• Number 5

The attacking member steps back with the left foot; performs a low block with the right hand and simultaneously *Ki Haps*. The senior member pulls the left leg back into fighting stance and *Ki Haps* in preparation for the rest of the exercise.

❶The defending member *Ki Haps*, signaling to the attacker that they are ready. The attacker steps forward with the right foot and performs a middle punch with the right fist. In response the defender performs a front kick with the right foot under the attacker's punch.

❷The defender then steps down with the right foot and immediately twists the hip completely to the left and performs an outside-inside block with the right hand. This block is done to insure defense after the kick.

❸Next the defender turns the hip over 90° to the right and performs a reverse high punch with left fist.

❹The defender then brings the left hand down and in doing this bring the attacker's fist down. This is done to clear the area and prepare for the next motion.

❺Next the defending member uses the left foot to perform an inside-outside kick. This kick is done with a simultaneous *Ki Hap*.

❻Immediately the defending member brings the left leg back behind the right leg and comes to fighting stance.

In closing, both members simultaneously return to *Ba Ro Jaseh* and bow. ■

• Number 6

The attacking member steps back with the left foot; performs a low block with the right hand and simultaneously *Ki Haps*. The senior member pulls the left leg back into fighting stance and *Ki Haps* in preparation for the rest of the exercise.

❶The defending member *Ki Haps*, signaling to the attacker that they are ready. The attacker steps forward with the left foot and performs a middle punch with the left fist. In response the defender performs a front kick with the left foot under the attacker's punch.

❷The defender then steps down with the left foot and immediately twists the hip completely to the right and performs an outside-inside block with the left hand. This block is done to insure defense after the kick.

❸Next the defender turns the hip over 90° to the left and performs a reverse high punch with right fist.

❹The defender then brings the right hand down and in doing this brings the attacker's fist down. This is done to clear the area and prepare for the next motion.

❺Next the defending member uses the right foot to perform an inside-outside kick. This kick is done with a simultaneously *Ki Hap*.

❻Immediately the defending member brings the right leg back behind the left leg and comes to fighting stance.

In closing, both members simultaneously return to *Ba Ro Jaseh* and bow. ■

4. Self Defense (*Ho Sin Sool*)
호신술

• Straight Hand #1

Both participants begin by bowing and finding a proper distance for the exercise. The attacker proceeds by using the right hand to grab the defender's left wrist.

❶The defender steps forward with the left leg into *Sa Ko Rip Jaseh,* moving the left arm over the attacker's right arm to break the hold.

❷Immediately the defender uses the left fist to perform a high back-fist strike to the attacker's face.

❸The defender, holding the same stance, then uses the left hand to perform a low hammer-strike to attacker's groin.

❹The defender then uses the right hand to perform a reverse ridge-hand attack to the attacker's temple. This technique is done with a *Ki Hap*.

In closing, both members bow and return to *Ba Ro Jaseh.* ▨

• Straight Hand #2

Both participants begin by bowing and finding a proper distance for the exercise. The attacker proceeds by using the right hand to grab the defender's left wrist.

❶The defender steps forward with the left leg into *Sa Ko Rip Jaseh.* While stepping, the defender's left hand holds onto the attacker's right wrist. Then raises the right hand preparing for the next motion.

❷Immediately use the right hand to perform a reverse knife-hand strike to the side of the attacker's neck. Then the defender wraps the right hand around the attacker's neck while keeping a firm grip on the attacker's right wrist.

❸While in this position, the defender uses the right knee to perform a knee kick to the attacker's stomach. This technique is done with a *Ki Hap*.

In closing, both members bow and return to *Ba Ro Jaseh*. ■

5. Breaking (*Kyo Pa*)
격파

• Step Behind Side Kick

▪ This technique delivers a powerful side kick while quickly closing the distance to an opponent.
▪ Strike the center of board with side of the heel and knife edge of foot.

GREEN BELT

GENERAL REQUIREMENTS
1. Sound moral character.
2. No age requirement, but must be a member of the Hwa Rang World Tang Soo Do Moo Duk Kwan Federation, in good standing.
3. Regular weekly Studio attendance.

Pyung Ahn Ee Dan
Page 120

GENERAL KNOWLEDGE
1. Conceptual knowledge of lower rank techniques.
2. Understanding of Moo Duk Kwan spirit by demonstrated attitude.
3. Additional knowledge of the basic techniques of Tang Soo Do.

Chil Sung #2
Page 126

DEMONSTRATION OF ABILITY
1. BASIC MOVEMENT (KEE CHO):
   <u>Hand techniques</u>: Soo Do middle block, Soo Do high block, two fist middle block, hand combinations incorporating above techniques.
   <u>Foot techniques</u>: 8 basic kicks, 3 basic jump kicks, jump roundhouse kick, and Flying Cobra kicks.

2. FORMS (HYUNG):
   Pyung Ahn Cho Dan, Pyung Ahn Ee Dan, Chil Sung Ee Roh Hyung, Hwa Rang Tournament Form #2

One Step Sparring
Page 134

3. ONE STEP SPARRING (IL SOO SIK DAE RYUN): #5 - 8, and 2 student creations

4. SELF DEFENSE (HO SIN SOOL): Cross-hand #1 - 4, Straight hand #1 - 4, Studio #1 - 6

Self Defense
Page 136

5. BREAKING (KYOK PA): Spinning Back Kick
   (Children under 10 will break a half-sized board.)

6. TERMINOLOGY:

Breaking
Page 138

Basic	기초 *Kee Cho*	Attack	공격 *Kong Kyuk*
Attention	차렷 *Cha Ryut*	Defense	막기 *Mahk Kee*
Bow	경넷 *Kyung Ret*	Form	형 *Hyung*
Begin	시작 *Si Jak*	Sparring	대련 *Dae Ryun*
Return	바로 *Ba Ro*	Endurance	인내 *In Neh*
Meditation	묵념 *Muk Nyum*	Humility	겸손 *Kyum Son*

평안이단

2. Pyung Ahn Ee Dan Hyung
Pyung Ahn 2 (29 movements)

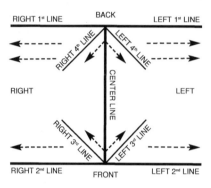

RIGHT 1ST LINE — BACK — LEFT 1ST LINE
RIGHT 4TH LINE — LEFT 4TH LINE
RIGHT — CENTER LINE — LEFT
RIGHT 3RD LINE — LEFT 3RD LINE
RIGHT 2ND LINE — FRONT — LEFT 2ND LINE

This *Hyung* follows the classic "I" format of the previous basic forms. It is the first time a kick is introduced into the traditional *Hyungs* and the first time a reverse technique is used. The introduction of these techniques shows the gradual progression of movement as the student develops. One of the more difficult techniques is the double middle and low block in the beginning portion of the *Hyung*. A series of movements that may challenge the coordination and balance of beginners are the series of reverse movements and front kicks performed in the later half of the *Hyung*. Remember this form follows the characteristic of the turtle, which includes calm confident movement.

Joon Bee Jaseh
Ready stance facing north

❶ *Hu Gul Yang Pal Mahk Kee*
(*Shi Sun:* Look to the left). Turn 90° to the left. Step out with the left foot and perform a *Hu Gul Yang Pal Mahk Kee* (Left middle block right high block).

❷ *Tuel Oh Ju Mok Kong Kyuk*
Pull the right hand down to the chamber with the bottom of the fist facing up. Perform a *Tuel Oh Ju Mok Kong Kyuk* (reverse uppercut to the chin) with the right fist.

❸ *Wheng Jin Kong Kyuk*
Extend right arm out to aim for the target Step forward with the left leg using an offensive hip turn and perform a *Wheng Jin Kong Kyuk* with the left fist.

④ *Hu Gul Yang Pal Mahk Kee*

(*Shi Sun*: Look over the right shoulder to the rear). Turn 180° to the right. Pull back the right leg and perform a *Hu Gul Yang Pal Mahk Kee*.

⑤ *Tuel Oh Ju Mok Kong Kyuk*

Pull the left hand down to the chamber with the bottom of the fist facing up. Perform a *Tuel Oh Ju Mok Kong Kyuk* with the left fist.

⑥ *Wheng Jin Kong Kyuk*

Extend left arm out to aim for the target. Step forward with the right leg using an offensive hip turn and perform a *Wheng Jin Kong Kyuk* with the right fist.

⑦ Pull left leg forward towards the center line back 90° and turn on the left leg. Pause for a moment in *Jun Gul Jaseh*. The right hand should be aiming to the south and the focus should be there as well. The left hand should be parallel to the ground and to the chest. It should be aiming to the south; aligned with the right hand. Simultaneously lift the right leg up back towards the left knee and bring both hands to the left chamber in preparation.

⑧ *Yup Cha Gi* (side kick)

Pause for a moment. Perform a *Yup Cha Gi* with the right hand extended out in a *Kwon Do Kong Kyuk* (hammer punch). *Ki hap*.

⑨ *Jung Dan Soo Do Mahk Kee* (middle knife hand block)

(*Shi Sun*: Immediately look over the the left shoulder to rear). Turn 180° to the left (north). Stepping out with the left foot and using a defensive hip turn, turn on the right performing a *Jung Dan Soo Do Mahk Kee* blocking with the left hand.

❿ *Jung Dan Soo Do Mahk Kee*
Stepping out with the right foot using a defensive hip turn; perform a *Jung Dan Soo Do Mahk Kee* blocking with the right hand.

⓫ *Jung Dan Soo Do Mahk Kee*
Stepping out with the left foot using a defensive hip turn; perform a *Jung Dan Soo Do Mahk Kee* blocking with the left hand.

⓬ *Kwan Soo Kong Kyuk*
(spear hand)
Step forward with the right leg using an offensive hip turn; perform a *Kwon Soo Kong Kyuk* with the right hand and simultaneously *Ki Hap*.

⓭ *Jung Dan Soo Do Mahk Kee*
(*Shi Sun*: Look over the left shoulder to the rear). Turn 270° to the left. Stepping out with the left foot, and turning on the right, perform a *Jung Dan Soo Do Mahk Kee* blocking with the left hand.

⓮ *Jung Dan Soo Do Mahk Kee*
(*Shi Sun*: Look to the right). Turn 45° to the right. Stepping out with the right foot, and turning on the left, perform a *Jung Dan Soo Do Mahk Kee* blocking with the right hand.

⓯ *Jung Dan Soo Do Mahk Kee*
(*Shi Sun*: Look over the right shoulder to the rear). Turn 135° to the right. Stepping out with the right foot, and turning on the left, perform a *Jung Dan Soo Do Mahk Kee* blocking with the right hand.

Back View

⓰ Jung Dan Soo Do Mahk Kee

(*Shi Sun*: Look to the left). Turn 45° to the left. Stepping out with the left foot, and turning on the right, peform a *Jung Dan Soo Do Mahk Kee* blocking with the left hand.

⓱ Tuel Oh Ahneso Pakuro Mahk Kee

(*Shi Sun*: Look to left). Turn 45° to the left stepping out with the left leg, while turning on the right, perform a *Tuel Oh Ahneso Pakuro Mahk Kee* (reverse inside outside block) with the right hand.

Back View

⓲ Ahp Cha Nut Gi

Perform an *Ahp Cha Nut Gi* (front thrust kick) with the right foot.

Back View

⓳ Tuel Oh Jung Dang Kong Kyuk

Stepping down with the right leg perform a *Tuel Oh Jung Dan Kong Kyuk* (reverse center punch) with the left hand.

Back View

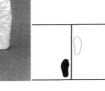

⓴ Tuel Oh Ahneso Pakuro Mahk Kee

While remaining in that stance perform a *Tuel Oh Ahneso Pakuro Mahk Kee* with the left hand.

Back View

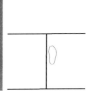

㉑ Ahp Cha Nut Gi

Perform an *Ahp Cha nut Gi* (front thrust kick) with the left foot.

㉒ Tuel Oh Jung Dang Kong Kyuk

Stepping down with the left leg perform a *Tuel Oh Jung Dan Kong Kyuk* with the right hand.

Back View

㉓ Sang Soo Jung Dan Mahk Kee

Step forward with the right leg using a defensive hip turn; perform a *Sang Soo Jung Dan Mahk Kee* (double reinforced inside outside center block) blocking with the right hand and simultaneously *Ki Hap*.

Back View

㉔ Ha Dan Mahk Kee

(*Shi Sun*: Look over the left shoulder to the rear). Turn 270° to the left. Stepping out with the left foot, and turning on the right, peform a *Ha Dan Mahk Kee* with the left hand.

㉕ Jung Dan Soo Do Mahk Kee

With a snap of the hip perform a one hand *Jung Dan Soo Do Mahk Kee* (middle knife hand block, or *kong kyuk* to the neck) with the left hand.

㉖ Sang Dan Mahk Kee

(*Shi Sun*: Look to the right). Turn 45° to the right. Stepping out with the right foot, and using a defensive hip turn, perform a *Sang Dan Mahk Kee* with the right hand.

㉗ Ha Dan Mahk Kee

(*Shi Sun*: Look to the right). Turn 135° to the right. Stepping out with the right foot, and turning on the left, perform a *Ha Dan Mahk Kee* with the right hand.

28 *Jung Dan Soo Do Mahk Kee*

With a snap of the hip perform a one hand *Jung Dan Soo Do Mahk Kee* (or *kong kyuk*) with the right hand.

29 *Sang Dan Mahk Kee*

(*Shi Sun*: Look to the left). Turn 45° to the left. Stepping out with the left foot, and using a defensive hip turn, perform a *Sang Dan Mahk Kee* with the left hand. *Ki hap.*

Ba Ro

Bring the left leg in and return to *Ba Ro Jaseh*.

2. Chil Sung Ee Roh Hyung
Chil Sung 2 (29 movements)

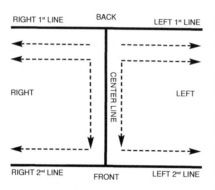

RIGHT 1st LINE   BACK   LEFT 1st LINE

RIGHT   CENTER LINE   LEFT

RIGHT 2nd LINE   FRONT   LEFT 2nd LINE

This form, created by Grand Master Hwang Kee, is peculiar not in it's performance or application but in the method in which it is usually taught. Notice that the first of the *Chil Sung* forms is taught to "Red Belts" but the second is taught to "Green Belts" and often times even to "Orange Belts". One wonders why the second form is introduced this way to students and why they were created with the second one being easier than the first. Regularly in the practice of *Hyungs*, the first form in a series is easier than the second or third, but in this series that is not the case. The *Chil Sung Hyung* should be used as a guide line for training. Pay attention to the transfer of motion between movements and the balance of internal and external power.

❶ *Ha Dan Mahk Kee*
(*Shi Sun:* Look to the left) Turn 90° to the left. Stepping out with the left foot and turning on the right perform a *Ha Dan Mahk Kee* with the left hand.

Joon Bee Jaseh
Ready stance facing north.

❷ *Tuel Oh Soo Do Kong Kyuk*
With a snap of the hip perform a *Tuel Oh Soo Do Kong Kyuk* with the right hand.

❸ *Moo Roop Cha Gi*
Raise the left hand to the level of the right, as if grabbing somebody by the shoulders. Perform a *Moo Roop Cha Gi* with the right knee. Simultaneously pull the hands down so that they pass over the knee.

④ *Jung Dan Kong Kyuk*
While aiming with the left hand step down with the right leg into *Jun Gul Jaseh* and perform a *Jung Dan Kong Kyuk* with the right fist.

⑤ *Tuel Oh Jung Dan Kong Kyuk*
Immediately with a snap of the hip perform a *Tuel Oh Jung Dan Kong Kyuk* with the left fist.

⑥ *Ha Dan Mahk Kee*
(*Shi Sun*: Look over the right shoulder to the rear). Turn 180° to the right. Stepping out with the right foot and turning on the left, perfom a *Ha Dan Mahk Kee* with the right hand.

⑦ *Tuel Oh Soo Do Kong Kyuk*
With a snap of the hip perform a *Tuel Oh Soo Do Kong Kyuk* with the left hand.

⑧ *Moo Roop Cha Gi*
Raise the right hand to the level of the left as if grabbing somebody by the shoulders. Perform a *Moo Roop Cha Gi* with the left knee. Simultaneouly pull the hands down so that they pass over the knee.

⑨ *Jung Dan Kong Kyuk*
While aiming with the right hand, step down with the left leg into *Jun Gul Jaseh*, performing a *Jung Dan Kong Kyuk* with the left fist.

❿ Tuel Oh Jung Dan Kong Kyuk
Immediately with a snap of the hip, perform a *Tuel Oh Jung Dan Kong Kyuk* with the right fist.

⓫ Ssang Soo Jung Dan Mahk Kee
(*Shi Sun*: Look to the left) Turn 90° to the left. Stepping out with the left foot, and turning on the right, peform a *Sang Soo Jung Dan Mahk Kee* with the left hand blocking.

⓬ Wheng Jin Kong Kyuk
While extending the left hand out for aim, step forward with the right leg using an offensive hip turn and perform a *Wheng Jin Kong Kyuk* with the right fist.

⓭ Wheng Jin Kong Kyuk
Step forward with the left leg using an offensive hip turn and perform a *Wheng Jin Kong Kyuk* with the left fist.

⓮ Wheng Jin Kong Kyuk
Step forward with the right leg using an offensive hip turn; perform a *Wheng Jin Kong Kyuk* and simultaneously *Ki Hap*.

⓯ Jung Dan Soo Do Mahk Kee
(*Shi Sun*: Look over the left shoulder to the rear) Turn 270° to the left. Stepping out with the left foot and turning on the right, peform a *Jung Dan Soo Do Mahk Kee* with the left hand blocking.

16 *Jung Dan Kong Kyuk*

Step forward with the right leg using an offensive hip turn, and perform a *Jung Dan Kong Kyuk* with the right fist.

17 *Jung Dan Soo Do Mahk Kee*

(*Shi Sun:* Look over the right shoulder to the rear). Turn 180° to the right. Step back with the right leg, turning on the left, and perform a *Jung Dan Soo Do Mahk Kee* with the right hand blocking.

18 *Jung Dan Kong Kyuk*

Step forward with the left leg using an offensive hip turn, and perform a *Jung Dan Kong Kyuk* with the left fist.

Back View

19 A. (*Shi Sun:* Look to left) Turn 90° to the left. Stepping out with the left leg while turning on the right; come to *Sa Ko Rip Jaseh* and cross both hands so that both palms are facing the body. The right hand should be over the left. The focus should remain to the South.
B. Without stepping, slowly change stance to *Jun Gul Jaseh* while simultaneously uncrossing the hands. The palms should be facing away from the body.

20 *Ahp Cha Nut Gi*

Simultaneously pull both hands back into fists, into the chamber and perform an *Ahp Cha Nut Gi* with the right foot.

Back View

Back View

21 A. Step down into *Sa Ko Rip Jaseh* and cross both hands so that both palms are visible. The left hand should be over the right. The focus should remain to the south.
B. Without stepping, slowly change stance to *Jun Gul Jaseh* while simultaneouly uncrossing the hands. The palms should be facing away from the body.

㉒ *Ahp Cha Nut Gi*
Simultaneously pull both hands back into fists, into the chamber and perform an *Ahp Cha Nut Gi* with the left foot.

Back View

㉓ A. Step down into *Sa Ko Rip Jaseh* and cross both hands so that both palms are visible. The right hand should be over the left. The focus should remain to the South. **B.** Without stepping, slowly change stance to *Jun Gul Jaseh* while simultaneously uncrossing the hands. The palms should be facing away from the body.

㉔ *Ahp Cha Nut Gi*
Leave the left hand out in *Soo Do* position for protecting, while pulling the right fist into the chamber. This should be done while performing an *Ahp Cha Nut Gi* with the right foot.

㉕ *Jung Dan Kong Kyuk*
Step down into *Jun Gul Jaseh* and perform a *Jung Dan Kong Kyuk* with the right fist and simultaneously *Ki Hap*.

㉖ *Hu Gul Ha Dan Mahk Kee*
(*Shi Sun*: Look over the left shoulder to the rear). Turn 270° to the left. Stepping out with the left foot and turning on the right peform a *Hu Gul Ha Dan Mahk Kee* with the left hand

㉗ *Sang Dan Kong Kyuk*
Step forward with the right leg using an offensive hip turn and perform a *Sang Dan Kong Kyuk* with the right fist.

28 *Hu Gul Ha Dan Mahk Kee*
(*Shi Sun*: Look over the right shoulder to the rear). Turn 180° to the right. Stepping out with the right foot and turning on the left peform a *Hu Gul Ha Dan Mahk Kee* with the right hand.

29 *Sang Dan Kong Kyuk*
Step forward with the left leg using an offensive hip turn, and perform a *Sang Dan Kong Kyuk* with the left fist.

Ba Ro
Bring the left leg in and return to *Ba Ro Jaseh*.

Applications for Pyung Ahn Ee Dan

Yang Pal Mahk Kee

Upper Cut

Soo Do Jung Dan Mahk Kee

Ahneso Pakuro Mahk Kee
& Ahp Cha Nut Ki

Wheng Jin Kong Kyuk

Applications for Chil Sung Ee Roh Hyung

Ha Dan Mahk Kee

Tuel Oh Soo Do Kong Kyuk

Moo Roop Cha Gi

Jung Dan Kong Kyuk

Ssang Soo Jung Dan Mahk Kee

Wheng Jin Kong Kyuk

Grabbing

Ahp Cha Nut Ki

Grabbing & *Ahp Cha Nut Ki*

Jung Dan Kong Kyuk

Hu Gul Ha Dan Mahk Kee

Sang Dan Kong Kyuk

3. One Step Sparring (*Il Soo Sik Dae Ryun*)
일수식 대련

• Number 7

The attacking member steps back with the right foot; performs a low block with the left hand and simultaneously *Ki Haps*. The senior member pulls the right leg back into fighting stance and *Ki Haps* in preparation for the rest of the exercise.

❶The defending member *Ki Haps*, signaling to the attacker that they are ready. The attacker steps forward with the right foot, and performs a middle punch with the right fist. In response the defender performs an outside-inside kick with the right foot blocking the attacker's punch. Without stepping down, the defender brings the right leg in toward the left knee in preparation for the next move.

❷The defender then performs a side-kick with the same leg.

❸Next the defender steps down with the right foot, performing a reverse high punch with the left fist.

❹The defender then brings the left hand behind the left side of the attacker's neck, pulling the head down while performing a left knee kick to the stomach.

❺Next the defending member steps down with the left foot and performs an elbow strike to the attacker's spine. This strike is done simultaneously with a *Ki Hap*.

In closing, both members return to *Ba Ro Jaseh* and bow. ▮

• Number 8

The attacking member steps back with the left foot; performs a low block with the right hand and simultaneously *Ki Haps*. The defending member pulls the left leg back into fighting stance and *Ki Haps* in preparation for the rest of the exercise.

❶The defending member *Ki Haps*, signaling to the attacker that they are ready. The attacker steps forward with the left foot and performs a middle punch with the left fist. In response the defender performs an outside-inside kick with the left foot blocking the attacker's punch. Without stepping down, the defender brings the left leg in toward the right knee in preparation for the next move.

❷The defender then performs a side-kick with the left leg.

❸Next the defender steps down with the left foot, performing a reverse high punch with the right fist.

❹The defender then brings the right hand behind the right side of the attacker's neck, pulling the head down while performing a right knee kick to the stomach.

❺Next the defending member steps down with the right foot and performs an elbow strike to the attacker's spine and simultaneously *Ki Haps*.

In closing, both members return to *Ba Ro Jaseh* and bow. ■

4. Self Defense (*Ho Sin Sool*)
호신술

• Straight Hand #3

Both participants begin by bowing and finding a proper distance at which to complete the exercise. The attacker proceeds by using the right hand to grab the defender's left wrist.

❶The defender flips his left wrist up and towards his body to allow room for the right hand to grab the attacker's wrist.

❷Immediately the defender steps with the left leg towards the right corner at a 45°, keeping a firm grip while extending both hands out. This motion is used to loosen the grip of the attacker and prepare for the next motion.

❸While keeping a firm grip on the attacker's right wrist, the defender turns clockwise to the right, pivoting on the right foot. Then defender steps under the attacker's right arm, stepping back with the right foot. Finally, pull both hands down to disable and gain control of the attacker.

❹While using the right hand to hold onto the attacker's wrist, the defender immediately uses the left fist to perform a high punch to the attacker's temple.

❺The defender uses the right leg to perform a round-house kick to the attacker's stomach. This technique is done with a *Ki Hap*.

In closing, both members bow and return to *Ba Ro Jaseh*. ■

• Straight Hand #4

Both participants begin by bowing and finding a proper distance at which to complete the exercise. The attacker proceeds by using the right hand to grab the defender's left wrist.

❶While keeping the left elbow close to the body, the defender turns the left hand around the attacker's right hand in a clockwise fashion. Apply pressure by pressing your thumb in between the attacker's first two knucles.
This motion is used to loosen the grip of the attacker and prepare for the next motion.

❷Using both hands the defender grabs the attacker's right wrist and places both thumbs on the back of the attacker's hand. While maintaining this hold the defender steps back with the right leg, pushing forward with both hands. This motion is used to make the attacker unstable, locking his arm and preparing for the next motion. The attacker's fingers should be pointing upward while the head should be facing the ground.

❸Without letting go of the attacker, the defender uses the right leg to perform a front snap-kick to the attacker's face.

❹Stepping down with the right leg into *Sa Ko Rip* stance, the defender performs a downward elbow strike to the back of the attacker's spine, all while maintaining control of the attacker. This last technique is done with a *Ki Hap*.

In closing, both members bow and return to *Ba Ro Jaseh*. ■

5. Breaking (*Kyo Pa*)
격파

• Spinning Back Kick

▪When half way through spin, look over shoulder to focus on center of board.
▪"Chamber" kicking leg, then drive kick through board.

GREEN BELT
WITH 1 STRIPE

GENERAL REQUIREMENTS
1. Sound moral character.
2. No age requirement, but must be a member of the Hwa Rang World Tang Soo Do Moo Duk Kwan Federation in good standing.
3. Regular weekly Studio attendance.

GENERAL KNOWLEDGE
1. Conceptual knowledge of lower rank techniques.
2. Understanding of Moo Duk Kwan spirit by demonstrated attitude.
3. Additional knowledge of the basic techniques of Tang Soo Do.

DEMONSTRATION OF ABILITY
1. BASIC MOVEMENT (KEE CHO):
    Hand techniques: two fist low and high block in Jun Gul Jaseh and Hu Gul Jaseh, and all previous hand combinations.
    Foot techniques: eight basic kicks, basic jump kicks, spinning crossing kick, kick combinations, Flying Cobra Kicks.

2. FORMS (HYUNG):
    Pyung Ahn Ee Dan, Pyung Ahn Sam Dan, Chil Sung Ee Ro Hyung, Hwa Rang Tournament Form #2

3. ONE STEP SPARRING (IL SOO SIK DAE RYUN): #7 - 10

4. SELF DEFENSE (HO SIN SOOL): Cross-hand #1 - 4, Straight hand #1-4, Two hand grip (one wrist) #1 & 2, Studio #1-4

5. BREAKING (KYOK PA): 2-point breaking: Reverse punch and stepping behind sidekick.
    (Children under 10 will break a half-sized board.)

6. FREE SPARRING (JA YU DAE RYUN)

7. SPECIFIC KNOWLEDGE OF CULTURE AND TERMINOLOGY:

Basic	기초	*Kee Cho*	Attack	공격	*Kong Kyuk*
Attention	차렷	*Cha Ryut*	Defense	막기	*Mahk Kee*
Bow	경넷	*Kyung Ret*	Form	형	*Hyung*
Begin	시작	*Si Jak*	Sparring	대련	*Dae Ryun*
Return	바로	*Ba Ro*	Endurance	인내	*In Neh*
Meditation	묵념	*Muk Nyum*	Humility	겸손	*Kyum Son*
			Honesty	정직	*Chung Jik*

Ettiquette: Why do you bow before you enter the Studio?

Pyung Ahn Sam Dan
Page 140

One Step Sparring
Page 147

Self Defense
Page 149

Breaking
Page 151

Free Sparring
Page 152

2. Pyung Ahn Sam Dan Hyung

평안 삼 단

Pyung Ahn 3 (27 movements)

RIGHT 1ˢᵗ LINE   BACK   LEFT 1ˢᵗ LINE

RIGHT   CENTER LINE   LEFT

FRONT

This form is one of the shortest forms in Tang Soo Do. Even if it is one of the shortest it will take time to consider and to understand the nature of all it's movements. The shape of the *Hyung* is more of an inverted "T" than the previous shape, "I". Some of the difficult moves include the double middle and low blocks, and the final jumping elbow strike. As with all the *Pyung Ahn Hyungs* the animal characteristic is the turtle. This means the *Hyung* should be done concentrating on stability and a strong defense.

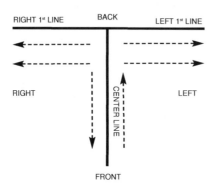

❶ *Yup Mahk Kee*
(*Shi Sun*: Look to the left). Turn 90° to the left. Step out with the left foot and perform a *Yup Mahk Kee* with the left hand.

Joon Bee Jaseh
Ready stance calm focused

❷ Without moving the left foot bring the right foot to the side of the left foot so that they are parallel and touching. The right hand should be in low block position and the left hand should be in middle block position, with the knees slightly bent.
Ha Dan & Jung Dan Mahk Kee
Simultaneously perform a right low block and a left middle block with the feet remaining together. The right hand should move inside the space between the right hand and the body. This should be done with a hip twist and immediately after step two.

A.

B.

❸ *Ha Dan & Jung Dan Mahk Kee*
Simultaneously perform a left low block and a right middle block with the feet remaining together. The left hand should move inside the space between the right hand and the body. This should be done with a hip twist.

④ Yup Mahk Kee (Shi Sun: Look over the right shoulder to the rear). Turn 180° to the right. Step out with the right leg and perform a *Yup Mahk Kee* with the right hand.

⑤ Without moving the right foot bring the left foot to the side of the right foot so that they are parallel and touching. The left hand should be in low block position and the right hand should be in middle block position, with the knees slightly bent.

Ha Dan & Jung Dan Mahk Kee Simultaneously perform a right low block and a left middle block with the feet remaining together. The right hand should move inside the space between the left hand and the body. This should be done with a hip twist.

⑥ Ha Dan & Jung Dan Mahk Kee Simultaneously perform a left low block and a right middle block with the feet remaining together. The left hand should move inside the space between the right hand and the body. This should be done with a hip twist and immediately after step five.

⑦ Ssang Soo Jung Dan Mahk Kee (*Shi Sun*: Look to the left). Turn 90° to the left. Stepping out with the left foot and turning on the right perform a *Ssang Soo Jung Dan Mahk Kee* with the left hand.

⑧ Kwan Soo Kong Kyuk Step forward with the right leg using an offensive hip turn and perform a *Kwon Soo Kong Kyuk* with the right hand. Short *Ki hap*.

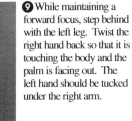

⑨ While maintaining a forward focus, step behind with the left leg. Twist the right hand back so that it is touching the body and the palm is facing out. The left hand should be tucked under the right arm.

🔟 Kwon Do Kong Kyuk
(*Shi Sun*: Immediately turn the head 360°). Continue stepping out with the left foot and perform a side *Kwon Do Kong Kyuk* with the left fist in *Kee Mah Jaseh*. Long *Ki hap*.

⓫ Jung Dan Kong Kyuk
Step forward with the right leg using an offensive hip turn; perform a *Jung Dan Kong Kyuk* and simultaneously *Ki Hap*.

⓬ (Shi Sun: Look over the left shoulder to the rear). Bring the left leg to the right leg while turning to the left 180° facing south. Cross the right arm over the left. Bring both hands to the side of the waist with the knees slightly bent. Now stand on the balls of the feet and come down so that the knees are straight. This should be done relatively slow.

Back View

⓭ Pakeso Ahnuro Cha Gi
Without any other movement perform a *Pakeso Ahnuro Cha Gi* with the right foot.

Back View

⓮ Jit Bal Kee
Stomp down with the right foot into *Kee Mah Jaseh*. Keep both hands at the waist.
Pal Koop Kong Kyuk
While keeping the focus to the south twist the hip into *Jun Gul Jaseh* so that the body is facing North. Simultaneously perform a *Pal Koop Kong Kyuk* with the side of the right elbow.

⓯ Kwon Do Kong Kyuk
Change stance into *Kee Ma Jaseh* and perform a *Kwon Do Kong Kyuk* with the right fist.

Back View

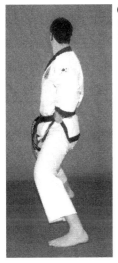

16 Immediately bring the right fist back so that both fists are at the waist.

17 *Pakeso Ahnuro Cha Gi*
Perform a *Pakeso Ahnuro Cha Gi* with the left foot.

Back View

18 *Jit Bal Kee*
Stomp down with the left foot into *Kee Mah Jaseh*. Keep both hands at the waist.
Pal Koop Kong Kyuk
While keeping the focus to the South twist the hip into *Jun Gul Jaseh* so that the body is facing North. Simultaneously perform a *Pal Koop Kong Kyuk* with the side of the left elbow.

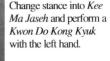

19 *Kwon Do Kong Kyuk*
Change stance into *Kee Ma Jaseh* and perform a *Kwon Do Kong Kyuk* with the left hand.

Back View

20 Immediately bring the left fist back so that both fists are at the waist.

21 *Pakeso Ahnuro Cha Gi*
Perform a *Pakeso Ahnuro Cha Gi* with the right foot.

㉒ Jit Bal Kee
Stomp down with the right foot into *Kee Ma Jaseh*. Keep both hands at the waist.
Pal Koop Kong Kyuk
While keeping the focus to the south twist the hip into *Jun Gul Jaseh* so that the body is facing North. Simultaneously perform a *Pal Koop Kong Kyuk* with the side of the right elbow.

㉓ Kwon Do Kong Kyuk
Change stance into *Kee Ma Jaseh* and perform a *Kwon Do Kong Kyuk* with the right fist.

Back View

㉔ Jung Dan Kong Kyuk
Step forward with the left leg using an offensive hip turn and perform a *Jung Dan Kong Kyuk* with the left fist.

Back View

㉕ While leaving the left fist out, bring the right foot to the left foot and step down into *Kee Mah Jaseh* facing the southern direction.

Back View

㉖ Sang Dan Kong Kyuk & Pal Koop Kong Kyuk
(*Shi Sun*: Look over the left shoulder to the rear). Turn 180° to the left. Stepping out with the left foot and turning on the right perform a *Sang Dan Kong Kyuk* with the right fist to the rear and a *Pal Koop Kong Kyuk* with the left elbow to the rear.

㉗ Sang Dan Kong Kyuk & Pal Koop Kong Kyuk
(*Shi Sun*: Look to the right). Jump to the right, simultaneously performing a *Sang Dan Kong Kyuk* with the left fist to the rear and a *Pal Koop Kong Kyuk* with the right elbow to the rear.
Ki hap.

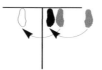

Ba Ro Jaseh
Pull the right leg in and
return to *Ba Ro Jaseh*.

Applications for Pyung Ahn Sam Dan

Ha Dan & Jung Dan Mahk Kee

Ssang Soo Jung Dan Mahk Kee

Kwan Soo Kong Kyuk

'right hand back'

Kwon Do Kong Kyuk

Jung Dan Kong Kyuk

Pakeso Ahnuro Cha Gi

*Jit Bal Kee
& Pal Koop Kong Kyuk*

Kwon Do Kong Kyuk

*Sang Dan Kong Kyuk
& Pal Koop Kong Kyuk*

3. One Step Sparring (*Il Soo Sik Dae Ryun*)
일수식 대련

• Number 9

The attacking member steps back with the right foot; performs a low block with the left hand and simultaneously *Ki Haps*. The senior member pulls the right leg back into fighting stance and *Ki Haps* in preparation for the rest of the exercise.

❶ The defending member *Ki Haps*, signaling to the attacker that they are ready. The attacker steps forward with the right foot and performs a middle punch with the right fist. In response the defender performs a front thrust kick with the right foot under the attacker's punch.

❷ The defender then steps back, turns to the right and performs a spinning back kick with the same leg.

❸ Next the defender steps down with the right leg and performs an inside outside knife hand block, blocking the attacker's punch. This block is done to insure defense after the kick.

❹The defender then uses the left fist to perform a reverse high punch to the face.

❺The defender will then bring the left hand down and in doing this bring the attacker's fist down. This is done to clear the area and prepare for the next motion.

❻Next the defending member jumps to the right corner at a 45° angle, performing a right palm strike to the base of the attacker's nose. This motion is done with a simultaneous *Ki Hap*.

In closing, both members return to *Ba Ro Jaseh* and bow. ■

• Number 10

The attacking member steps back with the left foot; performs a low block with the right hand and simultaneously *Ki Haps*. The senior member pulls the left leg back into fighting stance and *Ki Haps* in preparation for the rest of the exercise.

❶The defending member *Ki Haps*, signaling to the attacker that they are ready. The attacker steps forward with the left foot and performs a middle punch with the left fist. In response the defender performs a front thrust kick with the left foot under the attacker's punch.

❷The defender then steps back, turns to the left and performs a spinning back kick with the same leg.

❸Next the defender steps down with the left leg and performs an inside to outside knife hand block, blocking the attacker's punch. This block is done to insure defense after the kick.

❹The defender then uses the right fist to perform a reverse high punch to the face.

❺The defender brings the right hand down, and in doing this, brings the attacker's fist down. This is done to clear the area and prepare for the next motion.

❻Next the defending member jumps to the left corner at a 45° angle, performing a left palm strike to the base of the attacker's nose. This motion is done with a simultaneous *Ki Hap*.

In closing, both members return to *Ba Ro Jaseh* and bow. ■

4. Self Defense (*Ho Sin Sool*)
호신술

• Two to one Hand #1

Both participants begin by bowing and finding a proper distance at which to complete the exercise. The attacker proceeds by using the both hands to grab the defender's right wrist. It does not matter which hand is on top.

❶While keeping the elbow close to the body, the defender turns the hip completely to the left, directing the right hand downward. This first motion must be done while twisting the wrist in order to properly loosen the attacker's grip.

❷The defender then steps out 45⁰ to the right corner with the left leg while moving the right hand over the attacker's arms. The defender's left hand should follow to hold the attacker's elbow while it is bent. This motion should end with the defender using the right hand to hold the attacker's right wrist and the left hand to hold the attacker's right elbow straight and locked into position.

❸While maintaining the hold, the defender will perform a downward elbow strike to the attacker's triceps (right arm). This last technique is done with a *Ki Hap*.

In closing, both members bow and return to *Ba Ro* stance. ∎

• Two to one Hand #2

Both participants begin by bowing and finding a proper distance at which to complete the exercise. The attacker proceeds by using the both hands to grab the defender's right wrist. It does not matter which hand is on top.

❶The defender reaches over with the left hand between the attacker's two arms, grabbing the fingers of the right hand.

❷While moving into back-stance, right leg forward, the defender pulls the right hand from the grip of the attacker using the left hand. The hands are pulled back over the right shoulder to prepare for the next motion and ensure a clear line of sight.

❸ The defender simultaneously uses the left hand to deliver a high knife-hand strike to the attacker's neck, while using the right leg to perform a snap-kick to the attacker's groin.

❹ Using the right hand the defender performs a short vertical punch to the attacker's solar plexus. This final technique is done with a *Ki Hap*.

In closing, both members bow and return to *Ba Ro Jaseh*. ■

5. Breaking (*Kyo Pa*)
격파

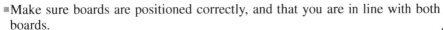

• Double Break - Middle Punch & Stepping Behind Side Kick

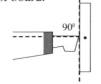

This style of breaking is to simulate fighting against two opponents. Multiple breaking should be executed as fast as possible.

- Make sure boards are positioned correctly, and that you are in line with both boards.
- Using hip and body power deliver middle punch to center of first board.
- Immediately look over your shoulder to focus on second board.
- Deliver a step behind side kick to center of board.
- Use hips to thrust through board.

6. Free Sparring Examples (*Ja Yu Dae Ryun*)
자유 대련

Back fist, Middle punch and Round House Kick

GREEN BELT
WITH 2 STRIPES

GENERAL REQUIREMENTS
1. Sound moral character.
2. No age requirement, but must be a member of the Hwa Rang World Tang Soo Do Moo Duk Kwan Federation, in good standing.
3. Regular weekly Studio attendance.

GENERAL KNOWLEDGE
1. Conceptual knowledge of lower rank techniques.
2. Understanding of Moo Duk Kwan spirit by demonstrated attitude.
3. Additional knowledge of the basic techniques of Tang Soo Do.

DEMONSTRATION OF ABILITY
1. BASIC MOVEMENT (KEE CHO):
   Hand techniques: Soo Do attacks, Yuk Soo Do attacks, Yuk Jin, hand technique combinations.
   Foot techniques: eight basic kicks, basic jump kicks, jump side kick, Yup Hu Ri Gi (Hook), flying cobra kicks, kick combinations.

2. FORMS (HYUNG):
   Pyung Ahn Sam Dan, Pyung Ahn Sa Dan, Chil Sung Ee Roh Hyung, Hwa Rang Tournament Form #2

3. ONE STEP SPARRING (IL SOO SIK DAE RYUN): # 9 - 12

4. SELF DEFENSE (HO SIN SOOL):
   Two hand grip (One wrist) #1 & 3, Two hand grip (both wrists) #1 & 2, Studio #1 - 8

5. BREAKING (KYOK PA):
   2-point breaking: knife hand and spinning back kick.

6. FREE SPARRING (JA YU DAE RYUN)

7. TERMINOLOGY:

Self defense	호신술	*Ho Sin Sool*
Breaking	격파	*Kyok Pa*
External Power	왜공	*Weh Gung*
Internal Power	내공	*Neh Gung*
Spiritual Power	심공	*Shim Gung*
Control of Power	힘조정	*Him Cho Chung*
Speed Control	완급	*Wan Gup*
Free Sparring	자유 대련	*Ja Yu Dae Ryun*
One-Step Sparring	일수식 대련	*Il Soo Sik Dae Ryun*
Tension and Relaxation	신축	*Shin Chook*

Pyung Ahn Sa Dan
Page 154

One Step Sparring
Page 160

Self Defense
Page 163

Breaking
Page 165

Free Sparring
Page 166

평안 사 단

2. Pyung Ahn Sa Dan Hyung
Pyung Ahn 4 (27 movements)

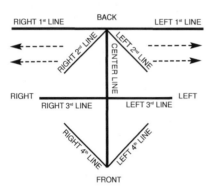

The fourth of the *Pyung Ahn* forms might be the most difficult to master. This is because of the wide variety of movements and the fact that many of the movements done in transition and performance are done on one leg. This wide variety of technique and difficult transition also make the form very pleasing to complete and or watch. As with all of the *Pyung Ahn* forms concentrate on balance and coordination; include peace of mind as well, these are attributes of the turtle.

Joon Bee Jaseh
Calm Passive *Yin*

❶ Jung Dan & Sang Dan Soo Do Mahk Kee
(*Shi Sun*: Look to the left). Turn 90° to the left. Step out with the left foot and perform *Jung Dan & Sang Dan Soo Do Mahk Kee* (middle knife hand block with the left hand & high knife hand block with the right hand).

❷ Jung Dan & Sang Dan Soo Do Mahk Kee
(*Shi Sun*: Look over the right shoulder to the rear). Turn 180° to the right. Perform a *Jung Dan & Sang Dan Soo Do Mahk Kee* (middle knife hand block with the right hand & high knife hand block with the left hand).

❸ Ha Dan Sang Soo Mahk Kee
(*Shi Sun*) Look to the left. Turn 90° to the left (north). Stepping out with the left foot and turning on the right perform a *Ha Dan Sang Soo Mahk Kee* (low double reinforced block).

❹ Sang Soo Jung Dan Mahk Kee
Stepping forward with the right leg, using a defensive hip turn, perform a *Sang Soo Jung Dan Mahk Kee* in *Hu Gul Jaseh*. Block with the right hand.

TRANSITIONS: A. Without switching stances reposition the arms. The right hand should be aiming to the west and the focus should be there as well. The left hand should be parallel to the ground and to the chest. It should be aiming west; aligned with the right hand.
B. Turn the head 90° to the left. Simultaneously lift the left leg up towards the right knee and bring both hands to the right chamber in preparation. Pause for a moment in *Han Bal Sogi Jaseh* (crane stance).

❺ Yup Cha Gi & Kwon Do Kong Kyuk
To the West perform a *Yup Cha Gi* with the left leg, with left hand extended out in a *Kwon Do Kong Kyuk*.

❻ Pal Koop Chi Ki
Step down with the left foot in *Jun Gul Jaseh*; simultaneously perform a *Tuel Oh Pal Koop Chi Ki* (right hand elbow strike with the left hand over the elbow).

❼ TRANSITION
(*Shi Sun*: Look over the right shoulder to the rear). Turn 180° to the right. Step out with the right foot into *Hu Gul Jaseh* and bring both hands to the left chamber.

TRANSITIONS:
A. Slide the left leg in, so that both legs are parallel facing North. The right and the left hand should be aiming to the east. The left hand should be parallel to the ground and to the chest.
B. Simultaneously lift the right leg up towards the left knee and bring both hands to the left chamber in preparation. Pause for a moment in *Han Bal Sogi Jaseh* (crane stance).

❽ Yup Cha Gi & Kwon Do Kong Kyuk
To the East perform a *Yup Cha Gi* with the right leg, with right hand extended out in a *Kwon Do Kong Kyuk*.

❾ Pal Koop Chi Kee
Step down with the right foot in *Jun Gul Jaseh*; simultaneously perform a *Tuel Oh Pal Koop Chi Kee* with the left hand (left hand elbow strike with the right hand over the elbow).

❿Tuel Oh Sang Dan Soo Do Kong Kyuk & Sang Dan Soo Do Mahk Kee
(*Shi Sun*: Look to the left). Twist the hip to the left and turn on both feet performing a *Tuel Oh Sang Dan Soo Do Kong Kyuk & Sang Dan Soo Do Mahk Kee* (reverse high knife attack with the right hand and high knife hand block with the left).

⓫ Ahp Cha Nut Gi
Without moving the position of the hands perform an *Ahp Cha Nut Gi* with the right foot.

⓬ Cap Kwon Kong Kyuk
Jump forward, perform a *Cap Kwon Kong Kyuk* with the right hand in *Kyo Cha Rip Jaseh*, and simultaneously *Ki Hap*.

⓭ TRANSITION
(*Shi Sun*: Look over the left shoulder to the rear). Turn 225° to the left. Bring both hands to the chamber. Stepping out with the left foot and turning on the right foot cross both hands together. The right hand should be on top of the left. Pull the hands apart so that they are one fist apart and at shoulder level. The final position should be in *Jun Gul Jaseh*.

Back View

⓮ Ahp Cha Nut Gi
While extending the left fist out for aim perform an *Ahp Cha Nut Gi* with the right leg.

⓯ Jung Dan Kong Kyuk & Tuel Oh Jung Dan Kong Kyuk
Step down and perform a *Jung Dan Kong Kyuk* with the right fist.

16 Tuel Oh Jung Dan Kong Kyuk
Immediately perform a *Tuel Oh Jung Dan Kong Kyuk* with the left fist.

17 TRANSITION
(*Shi Sun*: Look to the right). Turn 90° to the right. Bring both hands to the chamber. Stepping out with the right foot and turning on the left foot cross both hands together. The left hand should be on top of the right. Pull hands apart so that they are one fist apart and at shoulder level. The final position should be in *Jun Gul Jaseh*.

18 Ahp Cha Nut Gi
While extending the right fist out for aim perform an *Ahp Cha Nut Gi* with the left leg.

19 Jung Dan Kong Kyuk
Step down and perform a *Jung Dan Kong Kyuk* with the left fist.

20 Tuel Oh Jung Dan Kong Kyuk
Immediately perform a *Tuel Oh Jung Dan Kong Kyuk* with the right fist.

Back View

21 Sang Soo Jung Dan Mahk Kee
(*Shi Sun*: Look to the left). Turn 45° to the left. Stepping out with the left leg, using a defensive hip turn, perform a *Sang Soo Jung Dan Mahk Kee* in *Hu Gul Jaseh*. Block with the left hand.

㉒ Ssang Soo Jung Dan Mahk Kee
Stepping forward with the right leg, using a defensive hip turn, perform a *Ssang Soo Jung Dan Mahk Kee* in *Hu Gul Jaseh*. Block with the right hand.

㉓ Ssang Soo Jung Dan Mahk Kee
Stepping forward with the left leg, using a defensive hip turn, perform a *Ssang Soo Jung Dan Mahk Kee* in *Hu Gul Jaseh*. Block with the left hand.

Back View

㉔ Switching to *Jun Gul Jaseh* bring both hands up as if grabbing someone by the neck.

Back View

㉕ Moo Roop Cha Gi
Perform a knee attack with the right leg while bringing both hands down. The knee should pass through the hands. While doing this simultaneously *Ki Hap*.

Back View

㉖ Jung Dan Soo Do Mahk Kee
(*Shi Sun*: Immediately look over the left shoulder). Turn 225° to the rear. Immediately perform a *Sang Soo Jung Dan Soo Doo Mahk Kee* in *Hu Gul Jaseh*.

㉗ Jung Dan Soo Do Mahk Kee
(*Shi Sun*: Look to the right. Turn 45° to the right. Stepping out with the right foot and using a defensive hip turn perform a *Jung Dan Soo Do Mahk Kee* with the right hand blocking.

Ba Ro
Bring the right leg in and return to *Ba Ro Jaseh*.

Applications for Pyung Ahn Sa Dan

Yup Cha Gi & Kown Do Kong Kyuk

Pal Koop Chi Ki

Ahp Cha Nut Gi

Sang Dan Soo Do Kong Kyuk (or Stick Block) *& Sang Dan Soo Do Mahk Kee*

Sang Soo Jung Dan Mahk Kee

Moo Roop Cha Gi

Grabbing shoulders

3. One Step Sparring (*Il Soo Sik Dae Ryun*)
일수식 대련

• Number 11

The attacking member steps back with the right foot; performs a low block with the left hand and simultaneously *Ki Haps*. The senior member pulls the left leg back into fighting stance and *Ki Haps* in preparation for the rest of the exercise.

❶The defending member *Ki Haps*, signaling to the attacker that they are ready. The attacker steps forward with the right foot and performs a middle punch with the right fist. In response the defender performs a front kick with the left foot under the attacker's punch.

❷The defender then steps down, and uses the right leg to perform a roundhouse kick to the side of the attacker's head.

❸The defender steps down, turns to the left and performs a 'crescent kick' with the left leg.

❹The defender then steps back and performs a reverse middle punch with left fist. This punch is done with a simultaneous *Ki Hap*.

In closing, both members simultaneously return to *Ba Ro Jaseh* and bow. ■

• Number 12

The attacking member steps back with the left foot; performs a low block with the right hand and simultaneously *Ki Haps*. The senior member pulls the right leg back into fighting stance and *Ki Haps* in preparation for the rest of the exercise.

❶ The defending member *Ki Haps*, signaling to the attacker that they are ready. The attacker steps forward with the left foot and performs a middle punch with the left fist. In response the defender performs a front kick with the right foot under the attacker's punch.

❷ The defender then steps down, and uses the left leg to perform a roundhouse kick to the side of the attacker's head.

❸ The defender then steps down, turns to the right and performs a 'crescent kick' with the right leg.

❹ The defender then steps back and performs a reverse middle punch with right fist. This punch is done with a simultaneous *Ki Hap*.

In closing, both members simultaneously return to *Ba Ro Jaseh* and bow. ■

4. Self Defense (*Ho Sin Sool*)
호신술

• Two to one Hand #3

Both participants begin by bowing and finding a proper distance at which to complete the exercise. The attacker proceeds by using the both hands to grab the defender's right wrist. It does not matter which hand is on top.

❶ While keeping the elbow close to the body, the defender steps with the right foot to the left corner at a 45°. The defender continues moving the arms in an arching motion turning on the left foot, traveling counter clockwise underneath the attacker's right arm. Maintaining the hold while turning on the left foot, the defender turns to the left.

❷ Facing the attacker the defender is holding the attacker's right hand, so that the elbow is pointing upward. When the elbow is pointed up and the wrist is twisted it exposes what is commonly called the "floating rib". It is important to get the attacker into this position because it allows the ribs to be completely vulnerable to an attack.

❸ While maintaining the hold, controlling the attacker with the left hand, the defender performs a reverse middle punch to the "floating rib". This last technique is done with a *Ki Hap*.

In closing, both members bow and return to *Ba Ro* stance. ■

• Two to two Hands #1

Both participants begin by bowing and finding a proper distance at which to complete the exercise. The attacker proceeds by using the both hands to grab both wrists of the defender. It is done so that the attacker's right hand is holding the left hand of the defender and the left hand is holding the right hand of the defender.

❶ While keeping both elbows close to the body, the defender steps into front-stance with the right foot into the right corner at a 45° angle. While stepping, the defender brings both hands to the right side. In this position the right arm creates a right angle that is parallel to the shoulders and the left arm is parallel to the body and to the ground. This movement is designed to be performed very quickly so that the attacker's arms fly to the side, leaving an area of attack for the defender.

❷ Immediately the defender turns the hip 90° to the left and uses the right hand to perform a high knife-hand strike to the attacker's head and a low knife-hand strike to the attacker's rib area. This technique is done with a *Ki Hap*.

In closing, both members bow and return to *Ba Ro* stance. ■

• Two to two Hands #2

Both participants begin by bowing and finding a proper distance at which to complete the exercise. The attacker proceeds by using the both hands to grab both wrists of the defender. It is done so that the attacker's right hand is holding the left hand of the defender and the left hand is holding the right hand of the defender.

❶ While keeping the elbows close to the body the defender moves the left arm downward under the attacker's left arm.

❷ In a circular motion the defender raises both arms in this position. This move forces the attacker's arms to lock against each other at the elbow. The defender continues moving the left arm in a circular motion (counterclockwise) until the arms of the attacker are pinned against the attacker's body, completely breaking the attacker's grip. In this position the defender's right hand is raised to the ear in preparation for the next move and the left arm is used to hold the attackers arms against the body.

❸ The defender then turns the hip completely to the left into front stance while using the right hand to perform a high knife-hand strike to the attacker's head. This last technique is done with a *Ki hap*.

In closing, both members bow and return to *Ba Ro* stance. ■

Note: It is important that steps 2 and 3 are done quickly. To prevent the attacker from stepping back to regain freedom.

5. Breaking (*Kyo Pa*)
격파

• Double break - Knife Hand & Spinning Back Kick

This style of breaking is to simulate fighting against two opponents.
Multiple breaking should be executed as fast as possible.

- Make sure boards are positioned correctly, and that you are in line with both boards.
- Using hip and body power deliver knife hand strike to center of first board.
- Immediately look over your shoulder to focus on second board.
- Deliver a spinning back kick to center of board.
- Use hips to thrust through board.

6. Free Sparring Examples (*Ja Yu Dae Ryun*)
자유 대련

High Block, Palm Strike, Front Snap Kick and Inside-Outside Kick

RED BELT

Pyung Ahn Oh Dan
Page 168

GENERAL REQUIREMENTS
1. Sound moral character.
2. No age requirement, but must be a member of the Hwa Rang World Tang Soo Do Moo Duk Kwan Federation in good standing.
3. Regular weekly Studio attendance.
4. Service to the studio.

GENERAL KNOWLEDGE
1. Conceptual knowledge of lower ranks techniques.
2. Korean Tang Soo Do terminology, etiquette, and further development of Moo Duk Kwan attitudes and spirits.
3. Philosophy and history of Tang Soo Do Moo Duk Kwan.
4. Development of a leadership role and responsibility in the studio.

Chil Sung #1 *Page 174*

DEMONSTRATION OF ABILITY
1. **BASIC MOVEMENT (KEE CHO):**
   Hand techniques: All basics and combinations are required.
   Foot techniques: All basic foot techniques, spinning back kick, spinning hook kick, Bit Cha Gi (inside-outside thrust kick), flying tiger kicks.

2. **FORMS (HYUNG):**
   Pyung Ahn Sa Dan, Pyung Ahn Oh Dan, Chil Sung Il Ro Hyung, Hwa Rang Tournament Form #3 (recommended).

One Step Sparring
Page 185

3. **ONE STEP SPARRING (IL SOO SIK DAE RYUN):**
   # 11 - 14, 4 Student creations.

4. **SELF DEFENSE (HO SIN SOOL):**
   All Federation wrist grabs, Two hand grip (both wrists) #1 & 2 Studio #1 - 8

Self Defense *Page 187*

5. **BREAKING (KYOK PA):** Yup Hu Ri Gi (Hook kick)

6. **FREE SPARRING (JA YU DAE RYUN)**

7. **SPECIFIC KNOWLEDGE OF CULTURE AND TERMINOLOGY:**

   Terminology of Tang Soo Do movements.
   Ten Articles of Faith on Mental Training.
   Philosophy and history of Tang Soo Do Moo Duk Kwan.

Breaking *Page 189*

   Justice ....정의 *Jung Uei*
   Best Friendship ....의리 *Uei Rhee*

Free Sparring *Page 190*

2. Pyung Ahn Oh Dan Hyung
Pyung Ahn 5 (28 movements)

평안 오단

RIGHT 1ˢᵗ LINE — BACK — LEFT 1ˢᵗ LINE

RIGHT — CENTER LINE — LEFT

FRONT

This is the last of the *Pyung Ahn* forms. This form in particular contains many movements that are compact and close to the body which are characteristic of the turtle. One of the difficult moves is the jumping motion in the latter half of the form. Near the beginning of the form one of the complex movements is the *Yuk Jin Kong Kyuk*. While completing it motion try not to reveal to much of the body, thus leaving it open for attack.

A turtle symbolizes peace of mind, balance, control along with a good defense. One should practice with these things in mind.

❶ *Yup Mahk Kee*
(*Shi Sun*: Look to the left). Stepping out with the left foot and turning on the right, perform a *Yup Mahk Kee* with the left hand.

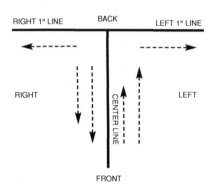

Joon Bee Jaseh

❷ *Yuk Jin Kong Kyuk*
Without changing stances perform a *Yuk Jin Kong Kyuk* (reverse middle punch not fully extended) with the right fist.

❸ Transition
(*Shi Sun*: Look to the right). Turn 90° to the right. Bring the right foot to the left foot so that they are parallel. Inhale. Bring both hands to the right chamber. Exhale slowly. The focus should be to the North as well as the position of the body.

④ Yup Mahk Kee
(*Shi Sun*: Look to the right). Turn 90° to the right. Stepping out with the right and turning on the left, perform a *Yup Mahk Kee* with the right hand.

⑤ Yuk Jin Kong Kyuk
Without changing stances perform a *Yuk Jin Kong Kyuk* (reverse middle punch not fully extended) with the left fist.

⑥ TRANSITION
(*Shi Sun*: Look to the left).
A. Turn 90° to the left. Bring the left foot to the right foot so that they are parallel. Inhale.
B. Bring both hands to the left chamber. Exhale slowly. The focus should be to the North as well as the position of the body.

⑦ Ssang Soo Jung Dan Mahk Kee
Stepping forward using a defensive hip turn use the right leg, perform a *Ssang Soo Jung Dan Mahk Kee* with the right hand blocking.

⑧ Ssang Soo Ha Dan Mahk Kee
Stepping forward with a defensive hip turn, perform a *Ssang Soo Ha Dan Mahk Kee*.

⑨ TRANSITION
Pull both hands back to the right chamber. The body should be in *Sa Ko Rip Jaseh* to prepare for the next motion.
Ssang Soo Sang Dan Mahk Kee
Without stepping forward use a hip twist and perform a *Ssang Soo Sang Dan Mahk Kee*.

**❿ *Soo Do Kong Kyuk &
Moo Roop Cha Gi***
As if grabbing a stick,
simultaneously bring both
hands down while bring-
ing the right knee up. The
right hand would be the
one grabbing the stick.
Perform a *Soo Do Kong
Kyuk* with the left hand
while performing a *Moo
Roop Cha Gi* with the
right knee.

⓫ *Jung Dan Kong Kyuk*
Step down with the right
leg and perform a *Jung
Dan Kong Kyuk* with the
right hand and simultane-
ously *Ki Hap*.

⓬ TRANSITION
(*Shi Sun*: Look over the
left shoulder to the rear).
Turn 180° to the left.
Turn on both feet and use
the right arm in a clearing
motion.
***Bal Ba Dahk Uro
Mahk Kee***
Immediately use the right
foot to perform a *Bal Ba
Dahk Euro Mahk Kee*
(outside inside block with
the foot).

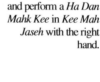

Back View

⓭ *Ha Dan Mahk Kee*
Immediately step down
and perform a *Ha Dan
Mahk Kee* in *Kee Mah
Jaseh* with the right
hand.

Back View

⓮ PREPARATION
(*Shi Sun*: Look over the
left shoulder to the rear).
Turn the head 180°.
Without changing stances
cross the hands so that the
left hand is in front of the
right.

Back View

**⓯ *Son Dung Kong
Kyuk***
In *Kee Mah Jaseh* per-
form a *Son Dung Kong
Kyuk* with the left hand.

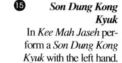

⑯ *Bal Ba Dahk Uro Mahk Kee*
Leave the left hand out and immediately perform a *Bal Ba Dahk Uro Mahk Kee* (outside inside block) with the right foot. While doing this strike extend the left arm in front and snap your right foot to your left hand. This technique can also be interpreted as offensive. In this case the extended arm grabs the attacker's head followed by the kick.

⑰ *Pal Koop Chi Ki*
Step down in *Kee Ma Jaseh* and perform a *Pal Koop Chi Ki* with the right elbow. The focus should be to the west.

⑱ *Cap Kwon Kong Kyuk*
With the left leg step behind the right leg in *Kyo Cha Rip Jaseh* and perform a *Cap Kwon Kong Kyuk* with the right fist. The left fist should be supporting the right arm at the elbow.

⑲ Transition
(*Shi Sun*: Look to the left and turn the head 180° to the left). Raise the right arm in an upward strike while stepping out with the left foot. The right leg should be straight with the left leg extended and toes pointed.

Back View

⑳ Jump
Step out with left leg; turn the body so that the focus is to the East. Jump up with the legs and arms crossed.

㉑ *Ssang Soo Ha Dan Mahk Kee*
Landing with the right leg in front crossing the right, perform a *Ssang Soo Ha Dan Mahk Kee*. This movement is done in a squatting *Kyo Cha Rip Jaseh*. Ki hap.

❷❷ *Ssang Soo Jung Dan Mahk Kee*
(*Shi Sun* : Look to the right). Turn 90° to the right. Step out with the right leg and perform a *Ssang Soo Sang Dan Mahk Kee* blocking with the right hand.

Back View

❷❸ *Ha Dan Kwon Soo Kong Kyuk*
(*Shi Sun*: Look over the left shoulder to the rear). Turn 180° to the left. Perform a *Ha Dan Kwon Soo Kong Kyuk* with the right hand. The left hand should be raised to the right shoulder but not touching.

❷❹ *Ha Dan Mahk Kee*
Pull the left leg back into *Hu Gul Jaseh*. With the right hand (pulling at the groin) pull back to the rear behind the head, while performing a *Ha Dan Mahk Kee* with the left hand to the front.

❷❺ TRANSITION
Without moving the hands pull the left leg toward the right leg so that they are parallel facing the East. Raise up on the toes then down again (slowly).

❷❻ *San Mahk Kee*
(**Mountain Block**)
Turn the body without moving the legs. The legs will cross with the right leg in back. The arms will cross with the left arm in front. Perform a *San Mahk Kee*.

❷❼ *Ha Dan Kwan Soo Kong Kyuk*
Perform a *Ha Dan Kwon Soo Kong Kyuk* with the left hand. The right hand should be raised to the left shoulder but not touching.

㉘ *Ha Dan Mahk Kee*
Pull the right leg back into
Hu Gul Jaseh. With the
left hand (pulling at the
groin) pull back to the rear
behind the head, while
performing a *Ha Dan
Mahk Kee* with the right
hand to the front.

Ba Ro
Bring the right leg back
and return to *Ba Ro Jaseh*.

칠성 일로 형

2. Chil Sung Il Roh Hyung
Seven Stars Form 1 (38 movements)

The *Chil Sung Hyungs* might be the most important *Hyungs* in all of Tang Soo Do. This is because the founder of Moo Duk Kwan, Grand Master Hwang Kee, created them during the 1980's. Considering the influence he has had on Tang Soo Do, the forms he has created should also be a great influence on any practitioner. Many of the movements are found only in the *Chil Sung Hyungs*. Grand Master Hwang Kee discovered many of the movements in an ancient Martial Arts text called *Mooye Dobo Tong Ji* (page 28). This text was studied by warriors at the time. The *Hyungs* should be practiced as a guideline for all who wish to become great warriors. This *Hyung* is representative of the seventh star of the Big Dipper, which is the North Star. World wide this constellation, and especially the North Star, is considered a guide for travelers. In ancient times travelers needed only to find the North Star to find their destination. In the same way, practitioners of Tang Soo Do should use the *Chil Sung* Forms as a guide for all of their training.

Chil Sung Il Ro Hyung is the first form that is almost entirely in *Neh Ga Ru*, meaning that the energy used is almost completely internal. This is evident in the slow graceful techniques and deep breathing. When completing this form concentrate on the transfer of air deep in the lungs along with the transfer of motion. It is important that *Ho Hop* (breathing) is done synchronously with the movements.

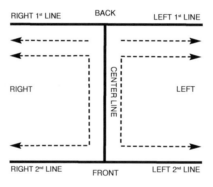

Joon Bee Jaseh
Ready stance, empty, waiting for a command. The focus should be to the North.

❶ TRANSITION (*Shi Sun*: Look to the left). Turn 90° to the left. Breathing In. Cross the arms so that the left arm is underneath the right. While Stepping out with the left foot into *Sa Ko Rip Jaseh*, spread the arms so that they are in a circular formation at shoulder heighth. Imagine holding a large bowl.

❷ Han Pal Ahn Uro Ahn Ko & Han Pal Son Bah Dak Uro Noo Roo Kee
Breathing out. Slowly. While slowly changing stances into *Jun Gul Jaseh* bring the left arm around into *Han Pal Ahn Uro Ahn Ko* (as if embracing with the left arm). While doing this move the right hand into *Han Pal Son Bah Dak Uro Noo Roo Kee* (this motion can serve as a groin strike or a low defense).

❸ Soo Do Kong Kyuk
Slowly breath in, the left hand should move over the right. While stepping into *Kee Mah Jaseh*, slowly breath out and perform a *Soo Do Kong Kyuk* with the left hand. The right hand should be level with the solar plexus and parallel to the ground. Let the body settle in this position.

❹ Jung Dan Kong Kyuk
Stepping forward with the right leg while using an offensive hip turn, perform a *Jung Dan Kong Kyuk* with the right hand.

❺ Hu Gul Ha Dan Yuk Soo Do Mahk Kee
(*Shi Sun*: Look over the left shoulder to the rear). Turn 180° to the right. Stepping out with the right foot and turning on the left perform a *Hu Gul Ha Dan Yuk Soo Do Mahk Kee*. The right leg should rest on the back of the heel, palms of hands face up.

❻ Soo Do Kong Kyuk
While slowly breathing in, the right hand should move over the left. While stepping into *Kee Mah Jaseh*, slowly breath out and perform a *Soo Do Kong Kyuk* with the right hand. The left hand should be level with the Solar Plexus and parralel to the ground. Let the body settle in this position.

❼ Jung Dan Kong Kyuk
Stepping forward with the left leg while using an offensive hip, perform a *Jung Dan Kong Kyuk* with the left fist.

❽ TRANSITION
(*Shi Sun*: Look to the left).
Turn 90° to the left. Cross
the arms so that the left
arm is underneath the
right. While stepping out
with the left foot into *Sa
Ko Rip Jaseh*, spread the
arms so that they are in a
circular formation at
shoulder heighth while
breathing in.

**❾ *Han Pal Ahn Uro Ahn Ko* &
*Han Pal Son Bah Dak Uro
Noo Roo Kee***
Slowly. While slowly changing
stances into *Jun Gul Jaseh* bring
the left arm around into *Han Pal
Ahn Uro Ahn Ko* (as if embracing with the left arm). While
doing this move the right hand
into *Han Pal Son Bah Dak Uro
Noo Roo Kee* (this motion can
serve as a groin strike or a low
defense). Breathe out during this
motion.

❿ *Yup Mahk Kee*
Stepping forward with a
defensive hip performing
a *Yup Mahk Kee* with the
right hand.

**⓫ *Jung Dan Soo Do
Mahk Kee***
Step forward with a
defensive hip and perform
a *Jung Dan Soo Do
Mahk Kee* with the left
hand.

⓬ *Wheng Jin Kong Kyuk*
Step forward with the
right leg using an offen-
sive hip turn; perform a
Wheng Jin Kong Kyuk
with the right fist and
simultaneously *Ki Hap*.

⓭ TRANSITION
(*Shi Sun*: Look over the left
shoulder to the rear). Turn 270°
to the left. Breathing in. While
stepping out with the left leg
into *Jun Gul Jaseh*, bring the
right arm over the head in an
arching motion to meet and
hold the left hand.
Immediately while keeping the
left leg straight fall back into *Hu
Gul Jaseh* while bringing hands
down then up to the solar plexus
in a scooping motion.

⓮ Settle in *Sa Ko Rip Jaseh* with the right hand holding the left. While changing stances to *Jun Gul Jaseh* slowly push out with both hands. While doing this breath out.

⓯ *Yang Pal Kyo Cha Soo Do Mahk Kee* Without changing stances cross the right hand over the left then uncross them so that the palms are completely facing inwards. Settle in this position.

⓰ *Ha Dan / Sang Dan Soo Do Mahk Kee* Changes stances into *Hu Gul Jaseh*. Pull the right hand back to the rear behind the head, while performing a *Ha Dan / Sang Dan Soo Do Mahk Kee* with the left hand to the front.

⓱ *Jung Dan Kong Kyuk* Stepping forward with the right leg and using an offensive hip, perform a *Jung Dan Kong Kyuk* with the right fist.

Back View

⓲ TRANSITION (*Shi Sun*: Look over the right shoulder to the rear). Turn 180° to the right. While stepping out with the right leg into *Jun Gul Jaseh*, breath in and bring the left arm over the head in an arching motion to meet and hold the right hand. Immediately while keeping the right leg straight, fall back into *Hu Gul Jaseh* and bring the hands down to block, then up to the solar plexus in a scooping motion.

⓳ Settle in *Sa Ko Rip Jaseh* with the left hand holding the right. While changing stances to *Jun Gul Jaseh*, slowly push out with both hands. While doing this breath out.

20 *Yang Pal Kyo Cha Soo Do Mahk Kee*
Without changing stances cross the left hand over the right then uncross them so that the palms are completely visible to you. Settle in this position.

21 *Ha Dan / Sang Dan Soo Do Mahk Kee*
Change stances into *Hu Gul Jaseh*. Pull the left hand back to the rear behind the head, while performing a *Ha Dan / Sang Dan Soo Do Mahk Kee* with the right hand.

22 *Jung Dan Kong Kyuk*
Stepping forward with the left leg, using an offensive hip, perform a *Jung Dan Kong Kyuk* with the left hand.

23 *Ha Dan Mahk Kee*
(*Shi Sun*: Look to the left). Turn 90° to the left. Stepping out with the left foot and turning on the right perform a *Ha Dan Mahk Kee* with the left hand.

Back View

24 *Jung Dan Soo Do Mahk Kee*
With a snap of the hip, perform a *Jung Dan Soo Do Mahk Kee* with the left hand.

Back View

25 *Jung Dan Kong Kyuk*
Stepping forward with the right leg using an offensive hip perform a *Jung Dan Kong Kyuk* with the right fist.

Back View

26 *Sang Dan Mahk Kee*
With a snap of the hip, perform a *Sang Dan Mahk Kee* with the right hand.

Back View

27 *Jung Dan Kong Kyuk*
Stepping forward with the left leg, using an offensive hip turn, perform a *Jung Dan Kong Kyuk* with the left fist.

28 *Sang Dan Mahk Kee*
With a snap of the hip, perform a *Sang Dan Mahk Kee* with the left hand.

Back View

29 TRANSITION
Aim to the target with the left fist.

Back View

30 *Jung Dan Kong Kyuk*
Step forward with an offensive hip to perform a *Jung Dan Kong Kyuk* and simultaneously *Ki Hap*.

Back View

31 *Yang Soo Ha Dan Noo Roo Kee*
Breathing in. Extend the left hand to the right, both palms should be facing south with palm down. While keeping the right leg straight, fall back into *Hu Gul Jaseh* and drop both hands to protect the groin area.

㉜ Yang Soo Jung Dan Jang Kwon Kong Kyuk
While slowly changing stance to *Sa Ko Rip*, bring both hands to their corresponding sides. Slowly changing stances to *Jun Gul Jaseh*, push out while breathing out.

㉝ Ssang Soo Jung Dan Mahk Kee
(*Shi Sun*: Look over the left shoulder to the rear). Turn 270° to the left and perform a *Ssang Soo Jung Dan Mahk Kee* with the left hand blocking.

㉞ Yang Soo Ha Dan Noo Roo Kee
Breath in. Extend the right hand to the left hand, both palms should be facing the west. While keeping the left leg straight, fall back into *Hu Gul Jaseh*, dropping both hands to protect the groin area.

㉟ Yang Soo Jung Dan Jang Kwon Kong Kyuk
While slowly changing stances to *Sa Ko Rip*, bring both hands to their corresponding sides. Slowly changing to *Jun Gul Jaseh*, push out while breathing out.

㊱ Ssang Soo Jung Dan Mahk Kee
(*Shi Sun*: Look over the right shoulder to the rear). Turn 180° to the right and perform a *Ssang Soo Jung Dan Mahk Kee* with the right hand blocking.

㊲ Yang Soo Ha Dan Noo Roo Kee
Breath in. Extend the left hand to the right hand, both palms should be facing the East. While keeping the right leg straight, fall back into *Hu Gul Jaseh*, dropping both hands to protect the groin area.

③⑧ Yang Soo Jung Dan Jang Kwon Kong Kyuk
While slowly changing stances to *Sa Ko Rip*, bring both hands to their corresponding sides. Slowly changing to *Jun Gul Jaseh* push out while breathing out.

Ba Ro Jaseh
Return to *Ba Ro Jaseh*.

Applications for Pyung Ahn Oh Dan

Yuk Jin Kong Kyuk

Ssang Soo Ha Dan Mahk Kee

Ssang Soo Sang Dan Mahk Kee

*Soo Do Kong Kyuk &
Moo Roop Cha Gi*

Ssang Soo Sang Dan Mahk Kee   Grabbing

Soo Do Kong Kyuk & Moo Roop Cha Gi   *Jung Dan Kong Kyuk*

Bal Ba Dahk Uro Mahk Kee   *Cap Kwon Mahk Kee*   Upward Strike
                        (or *Cap Kwon Kong Kyuk*)

Jump

Ssang Soo Ha Dan Mahk Kee

Ha Dan Kwon Soo Kong Kyuk

San Mahk Kee

Applications for Chil Sung Il Roh Hyung

Han Pal Ahn Uro Ahn Ko & Han Pal Son Bah Dak Uro Noo Roo Kee

Soo Do Kong Kyuk

Jung Dan Kong Kyuk

Bringing hands down & *Mahk Kee* (block)

Pushing out & *Kong Kyuk*

Yang Pal Kyo Cha Soo Do Mahk Kee

Ha Dan Mahk Kee

Jung Dan Soo Do Kong Kyuk

Yang Soo Ha Dan Noo Roo Kee

Ssang Soo Jung Dan Jang Kwon Kong Kyuk

3. One Step Sparring (*Il Soo Sik Dae Ryun*)
일수식 대련

- Number 13

The attacking member steps back with the right foot; performs a low block with the left hand and simultaneously *Ki Haps*. The senior remains in *Joon Bee Jaseh* in preparation for the rest of the exercise.

❶ The defending member *Ki Haps*, signaling to the attacker that they are ready. The attacker steps forward with the right foot and performs a middle punch with the right fist. In response the defender steps to the left corner at a 45⁰ with the left leg. The defender turns into a back stance and uses the right hand to perform an inside-outside knife hand block.

❷ Using the right hand to grab the attacker's wrist, the defender uses the right leg to perform a roundhouse kick to the attacker's mid-section.

❸ The defender then steps down and uses the right leg to perform an inside-outside kick to the attacker's head.

❹ The defender steps down next to the left foot and performs a sweeping motion with the left leg. This sweeping motion is done while holding the attacker's chest.

❺ Next the defender turns to the left where the attacker is lying and uses the right fist to perform a low reverse punch to the attacker's face. This punch is done with a simultaneous *Ki Hap*.

In closing, both members return to *Ba Ro Jaseh* and bow. ■

• Number 14

The attacking member steps back with the left foot; performs a low block with the right hand and simultaneously *Ki Haps*. The senior remains in *Joon Bee Jaseh* in preparation for the rest of the exercise.

❶ The defending member *Ki Haps*, signaling to the attacker that they are ready. The attacker steps forward with the left foot and performs a high punch with the left fist. In response the defender steps to the right corner at a 45⁰ with the right leg. The defender turns into back stance, using the left hand to perform an inside-outside knife hand block.

❷ Using the left hand to grab the attacker's wrist, the defender uses the left leg to perform a roundhouse kick to the attacker's mid-section.

❸ The defender steps down and uses the left leg to perform an inside-outside kick to the attacker's head.

❹ The defender steps down next to the right foot and performs a sweeping motion with the right leg. This sweeping motion is done while holding the attacker's chest.

❺ Next the defender turns to the right where the attacker is lying and uses the left fist to perform a low reverse punch to the attacker's face. This punch is done with a simultaneous *Ki Hap*.

In closing, both members simultaneously return to *Ba Ro Jaseh* and bow. ■

4. Self Defense (*Ho Sin Sool*)
호신술

- Two to two Hands #3

   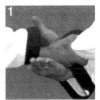

Both participants begin by bowing and finding a proper distance at which to complete the exercise. The attacker proceeds by using the both hands to grab both wrists of the defender. It is done so that the attacker's right hand is holding the left hand of the defender and the left hand is holding the right hand of the defender.

❶ The defender flips the left wrist toward the body to allow room for the right hand to grab the attacker's wrist.

❷ Immediately the defender steps with the left leg towards the right corner at a 45°, keeping a firm grip while extending both hands out. This motion is used to loosen the grip of the attacker and prepare for the next motion.

❸ While keeping a firm grip on the attacker's right wrist, the defender turns clockwise to the right, pivoting on the right foot. Then defender steps under the attacker's right arm and steps back with the right foot. Finally, the defender pulls both hands down to lock-up the attacker's arm and gaining control.

❹ While using the right hand to hold onto the attacker's wrist, the defender immediately uses the left fist to perform a high punch to the attacker's temple.

❺ The defender uses the right leg to perform a round-house kick with the ball of the foot to the attacker's stomach. This technique is done with a *Ki Hap*.

In closing, both members bow and return to *Ba Ro Jaseh*. ∎

• Two to two Hands #4

Both participants begin by bowing and finding a proper distance at which to complete the exercise. The attacker proceeds by using the both hands to grab both wrists of the defender. It is done so that the attacker's right hand is holding the left hand of the defender and the left hand is holding the right hand of the defender.

❶ While keeping both elbows close to the body, the defender steps to the side while turning the hip 45° to the left, and directs the right hand downward. This first motion must be done while twisting the wrist in order to properly loosen the attacker's grip. Before completing the motion the left hand is directed upwards grabbing the attackers left wrist and completely freeing it from the hold.

❷ While maintaining the hold on the attacker's wrist, the defender uses the right wrist to perform a low wrist strike to the attacker's groin.

❸ Using both hands to hold onto the attacker's left wrist, the defender steps clockwise with the left foot to the right corner at 45° and continues turning to the right while pivoting on the right foot until facing the attacker. In this position the attacker's left elbow should be pointing upwards.

❹While maintaining the hold with the right hand, the defender uses the left fist to perform a middle punch to the "floating-rib". This technique is done with a *Ki Hap*.

In closing both members bow and return to *Ba Ro Jaseh*. ∎

5. Breaking (*Kyo Pa*)
격파

• Hook Kick

■ While focusing on board in fighting stance, step behind and chamber kicking foot.
■ Drive through board with heel of foot.

Back View

6. Free Sparring Examples (*Ja Yu Dae Ryun*)
자유 대련

Back Fist, Reverse Middle Punch, Front Thrust Kick, and without dropping the leg, Round House Kick to the face with left foot.

RED BELT
WITH 1 STRIPE

GENERAL REQUIREMENTS
1. Sound moral character.
2. No age requirement, but must be a member of the Hwa Rang World Tang Soo Do Moo Duk Kwan Federation in good standing.
3. Regular weekly Studio attendance.
4. Service to the studio.

Bassai
Page 192

GENERAL KNOWLEDGE
1. Conceptual knowledge of lower rank techniques.
2. Korean Tang Soo Do terminology, etiquette, and further development of Moo Duk Kwan attitudes and spirits.
3. Philosophy and history of Tang Soo Do Moo Duk Kwan.
4. Development of a leadership role and responsibility in the studio.

One Step Sparring
Page 204

DEMONSTRATION OF ABILITY
1. **BASIC MOVEMENT (KEE CHO):**
   <u>Hand techniques:</u> All basics and combinations are required, with emphasis on Tuel Oh (Twisting) defenses and offenses.
   <u>Foot techniques:</u> All single jump kicks required, plus hand and foot combinations.

2. **FORMS (HYUNG):**
   Pyung Ahn Oh Dan, Bassai, Chil Sung Il Roh Hyung, Hwa Rang Tournament Form #3 (recommended).

Self Defense
Page 207

3. **ONE STEP SPARRING (IL SOO SIK DAE RYUN):**
   # 13 - 16, 4 Student creations.

4. **SELF DEFENSE (HO SIN SOOL):** Cross hand sleeve grabs # 1 - 2

5. **BREAKING (KYOK PA):**
   2-point breaking: Stepping behind side kick and hook kick

6. **FREE SPARRING (JA YU DAE RYUN)**

7. **SPECIFIC KNOWLEDGE OF CULTURE AND TERMINOLOGY:**
   Terminology of Tang Soo Do Movements.
   Ten Articles of Faith on Mental Training.
   Philosophy and History of Tang Soo Do Moo Duk Kwan.

Breaking
Page 209

8. **MOO DUK KWAN SAMPLE QUESTION:**
   Ten Key Concepts: Why are these important?

Free Sparring
Page 210

밧사이 2. Bassai
(52 movements)

RIGHT 1st LINE   BACK   LEFT 1st LINE

RIGHT   CENTER LINE   LEFT

FRONT

In a different era *Bassai Hyung* was called *Pal Che Dae* and it had a counter part called *Pal Che So*. They were the "lesser and greater selection of the best choice". *Bassai Hyung* is different than *Pyung Ahn Hyungs*. *Pyung Ahn Hyungs* are done with a calm and peaceful mind like a turtle but the characteristic of *Bassai Hyung* is a snake so the movement has to be quicker and smoother. It uses lower stances and strikes to the lower levels. It also uses more double striking, hand and feet combinations. *Bassai Hyung* demonstrates how to fight with multiple attackers because it turns, while blocking and striking. Advanced "Red Belts" and "Black Belts" perform *Bassai Hyung*.

❶ Beginning from *Joon Bee Jaseh* switch to **Bassai Joon Bee Jaseh** stance in preparation for the *Hyung*.

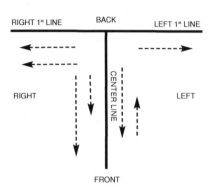

❷ *Ahneso Pakuro Mahk Kee*
Jump forward, land in *Kyo Cha Rip Jaseh* and perform an *Ahneso Pakuro* with the right fist. The focus should be to the North with the direction of the body to the west. The left foot should behind the right with the left hand supporting the right at the wrist.

❸ *Ahneso Pakuro Mahk Kee*
(*Shi Sun*: Look over the left shoulder to the rear). Turn 180° to the left. Step out with the left foot and perform an *Ahneso Pakuro Mahk Kee* with the left hand.

Back View

❹ *Tuel Oh Ahneso Pakuro Mahk Kee*
Without changing stances, use a hip twist and perform a *Tuel Oh Ahneso Pakuro Mahk Kee*.

❺ *Tuel Oh Pakeso Ahnuro Mahk Kee*
(*Shi Sun*: Look over the right shoulder to the rear). Turn 180° to the right. While turning on both feet, perform a *Tuel Oh Pakeso Ahnuro Mahk Kee* with the left hand.

❻ *Ahneso Pakuro Mahk Kee*
Without changing stances, use a hip twist and perform an *Ahneso Pakuro Mahk Kee* with the right hand.

❼ *Ha Dan Mahk Kee*
Without turning the body, lift the right leg up into *Han Bal Sogi Jaseh* and perform a *Ha Dan Mahk Kee* in the Eastern direction.

❽ *Pakeso Ahnuro Mahk Kee*
(*Shi Sun*: Look to the right). Immediately, while keeping the focus to the East, turn the body 90° to the East; step down in *Jun Gul Jaseh* and perform a *Pakeso Ahnuro Mahk Kee* with the right hand.

❾ *Tuel Oh Ahneso Pakuro Mahk Kee*
Without changing stances, use a hip twist and perform a *Tuel Oh Ahneso Pakuro Mahk Kee* with the left hand.

Note: Steps 6 through 9 should be done with an emphasis on fluidity.

⑩ TRANSITION
(*Shi Sun*: Look to the left). Turn 90° to the left. While turning into *Kee Mah Jaseh* Move the left hand over the right hand so that it is parallel with the body and the ground. The right hand should be straightened in front of the body and parallel with the ground. The body's direction and the focus should both be to the North. Slowly draw the right fist into the chamber while simultaneously making the left hand a fist.

⑪ *Soo Do Kong Kyuk*
While remaining in *Kee Mah Jaseh* perform a *Soo Do Kong Kyuk* with the left hand.

⑫ *Jung Dan Kong Kyuk*
Without changing stances use a hip twist and perform a *Jung Dan Kong Kyuk* with the right fist.

⑬ *Ahneso Pakuro Mahk Kee*
While turning on both feet into *Jun Gul Jaseh*, perform an *Ahneso Pakuro Mahk Kee* with the right hand. The body should be facing the West with the focus and the direction of the block to the North.

⑭ *Jung Dan Kong Kyuk*
While turning on both feet into *Kee Mah Jaseh* perform a *Jung Dan Kong Kyuk* with the left fist. The body should be facing the North along with the focus and the direction of the punch.

⑮ *Ahneso Pakuro Mahk Kee*
While turning on both feet into *Jun Gul Jaseh*, perform an *Ahneso Pakuro Mahk Kee* with the left hand. The body should be facing the East with the focus and the direction of the block to the North.

16 *Soo Do Jung Dan Mahk Kee*
Step forward with the right leg using a defensive hip, and perform a *Soo Do Jung Dan Mahk Kee* with the right hand.

17 *Soo Do Jung Dan Kong Kyuk*
Step forward with the left leg using a defensive hip turn, and perform a *Soo Do Jung Dan Mahk Kee* with the left hand.

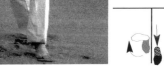

18 *Soo Do Jung Dan Kong Kyuk*
Step forward with the right leg using a defensive hip turn, and perform a *Soo Do Jung Dan Kong Kyuk* with the right hand.

19 *Hu Jin (stepping back) Soo Do Mahk Kee*
Step back with the right foot into *Hu Gul Jaseh* and perform a *Soo Do Mahk Kee.* This block should be done by crossing the left hand over the right.

20 *Soo Do Sang Dan Mahk Kee*
Step into *Kyo Cha Rip Jaseh*; the left foot should be in front of the right. Simultaneously perform a *Soo Do Sang Dan Mahk Kee* with the right hand while bringing the left hand up to meet the right. When completed, the left hand should be holding the right with the focus to the North.

21 *Yup Podo Cha Gi*
Perform a *Yup Podo Cha Gi* with the right foot and simultaneously *Ki Hap.*

㉒ *Jung Dan Soo Do Mahk Kee*
(*Shi Sun*: Look over the left shoulder to the rear). Turn 180⁰ to the left. Step down from the kick into *Hul Gul Jaseh*, and perform a *Jung Dan Soo Do Mahk Kee* with the left hand.

Back View

㉓ *Jung Dan Soo Do Mahk Kee*
Step forward with the right foot using a defensive hip, and perform *Jung Dan Soo Do Mahk Kee* with the right hand.

TRANSITION
While bringing hands down into fists, bring the right foot back so that it is touching and parallel with the left. The hands should be down near the hips similar to what may look like a double low block.
㉔ *Yang Pal Sang Dan Mahk Kee*
Without stepping, bring the hands into chest level. Perform a *Yang Pal Sang Dan Mahk Kee* (Double arm high block).

Back View

㉕ *Yang Soo Kwon Do Kong Kyuk*
Step forward with the right leg and perform a *Yang Soo Kwon Do Kong Kyuk* (double hammer strike to the middle region).

Back View

㉖ *Ee Dan Seh Bon Kong Kyuk*
Extend the left hand out for aim. Jump forward and perform two punches, first with the right then with the left (#27).

Back View

㉗ Left Punch.

28 Land in *Jun Gul Jaseh*. Perform a **Jung Dan Kong Kyuk** with the right hand. *Ki Hap*.

Note: Steps 24 through 28 should be done with an emphasis on fluidity.

29 *Ha Dan Kwon Soo Kong Kyuk*
(*Shi Sun*: Look over the left shoulder to the rear). Turn 180° to the left. Perform a *Ha Dan Kwon Soo Kong Kyuk* with the right hand. The left hand should be raised to the right shoulder but not touching.

30 *Ha Dan Mahk Kee*
Pull the left leg back into *Hu Gul Jaseh*, while uncrossing both hands. The right hand pulls back to the rear behind the head, while performing a *Ha Dan Mahk Kee* with the left hand to the front.

31 TRANSITION
Without moving the hands pull the left leg toward the right leg so that they are parallel facing the East. Raise up on the toes then down again (slowly).

32 *Bal Ba Dahk Uro Mahk Kee*
Bring the right arm forward to help direct the body. Perform a *Bal Ba Dahk Uro Mahk Kee* with the right foot.

33 *Ha Dan Mahk Kee*
Immediately step down and perform a *Ha Dan Mahk Kee* in *Kee Mah Jaseh* with the right hand.

34 Son Dung Kong Kyuk
(*Shi Sun*: Look over the left shoulder to the rear). Turn the head 180°. Without changing stances cross the hands so that the left hand is in front of the right. In *Kee Mah Jaseh* perform a *Son Dung Kong Kyuk* (strike with the back of the hand) with the left hand.

Back View

35 Bal Ba Dahk Uro Mahk Kee
Leave the left hand out and immediately perform a *Bal Ba Dahk Uro Mahk Kee* (outside inside block) with the right foot. While doing this strike the left hand with the right foot.

Back View

36 Pal Koop Che Ki
Step down in *Kee Muh Jaseh* and perform a *Pal Koop Che Ki* with the right hand. The focus should be to the west.

37 Ha Dan Mahk Kee
Without changing stances, move the right hand under the left hand to perform a *Ha Dan Mahk Kee* with the right hand. The left arm should be parallel with the body, with the palm facing down.

38 Ha Dan Mahk Kee
Without changing stances, move the left hand under the right hand to perform a *Ha Dan Mahk Kee* with the left hand. The right arm should be parallel with the body, with the palm facing down.

39 Ha Dan Mahk Kee
Without changing stances, move the right hand under the left hand to perform a *Ha Dan Mahk Kee* with the right hand. The left arm should be parallel with the body, with the palm facing down.

40 TRANSITION

(*Shi Sun*: Look to the right). Turn 90° to the right. Step out with the right foot and turning on the left into *Jun Gul Jaseh*. Bring both hands to the left side; with the left hand in the left chamber and the right hand parallel with the body.

41 *Yang Pal Kong Kyuk*

With the snap of the hip perform a *Yang Pal Mahk Kee* in *Jun Gul Jaseh*. The left hand should be performing a high punch, with the right hand performing a middle punch.

Back View

Back View

42 TRANSITIONS

A. Bring the right foot back so that it is touching and parallel with the left. Bring both hands to the left side; with the left hand in the left chamber and the right hand parallel with the body.
B. Raise the body up on the toes while extending both fists out. Slowly lower the body and bring both hands to the right side; with the right hand in the right chamber and the left hand parallel with the body.

Back View

43 *Bal Ba Dahk Uro Mahk Kee*

Perform a *Bal Ba Dahk Uro Mahk Kee* with the left foot.

Back View

44 *Yang Pal Kong Kyuk*

Step down into *Jun Gul Jaseh* and perform a *Yang Pal Mahk Kee*. The right hand should be performing a high punch, with the left hand performing a middle punch.

45 TRANSITIONS:

A. Bring the left foot back so that it is touching and parallel with the right. Bring both hands to the right side; with the right hand in the right chamber and the left hand parallel with the body.
B. Raise the body up on the toes while extending both fists out. Slowly lower the body and bring both hands to the left side; with the left hand in the left chamber and the right hand parallel with the body.

❹⑥ Bal Ba Dahk Uro Mahk Kee
Perform a *Bal Ba Dahk Uro Mahk Kee* with the right foot.

Back View

❹⑦ Yang Pal Kong Kyuk
Step down into *Jun Gul Jaseh* and perform a *Yang Pal Kong Kyuk*. The left hand should be performing a high punch, with the right hand performing a middle punch.

Back View

TRANSITION
(*Shi Sun*: Look over the left shoulder the rear). Turn 270° to the left. Step out with the left foot and turn on the right foot into *Choi Ha Dan Jun Gul Jaseh* (lowest front stance). The focus should be to the North with the body facing the West. Perform a sweeping motion with the right hand coming from outside to inside.

❹⑧ Choi Ha Dan Jun Gul Jaseh Cap Kwon Kong Kyuk
Without changing stances perform a *Choi Ha Dan Cap Kwon Kong Kyuk* (lowest *Cap Kwon Kong*) with the right fist.

TRANSITION
Turn on both feet into *Choi Ha Dan Jun Gul Jaseh* (lowest front stance). The focus should be to the North with the body facing the East. Perform a sweeping motion with the left hand coming from outside to inside.

❹⑨ Choi Ha Dan Jun Gul Jaseh Cap Kwon Kong Kyuk
Without changing stances perform a *Choi Ha Dan Cap Kwon Kong Kyuk* (lowest *Cap Kwon Kong*) with the left fist.

50 *Soo Do Jung Dan Mahk Kee*
Step toward the center with the left foot then step forward with the right foot into *Soo Do Jung Dan Mahk Kee.*

51 *Soo Do Jung Dan Mahk Kee*
(*Shi Sun:* Look to the right). Turn 90° to the right. Stepping out with the right foot and turning on the left perform a *Soo Do Jung Dan Mahk Kee* with the right hand.

52 *Soo Do Jung Dan Mahk Kee*
(*Shi Sun:* Look to the left). Turn 90° to the left. Stepping out with the left foot and turning on the right perform a *Soo Do Jung Dan Mahk Kee* with the left hand blocking. Simultaneously *Ki Hap.*

Ba Ro
Return to *Bassai Joon Bee* by stepping back with the left foot, then finish in *Ba Ro* Jaseh.

Ahneso Pakuro Mahk Kee

Ahneso Pakuro Mahk Kee

Ha Dan Mahk Kee

Pakeso Ahnuro Mahk Kee

Soo Do Jung Dan Mahk Kee

Soo Do Sang Dan Mahk Kee

Yup Cha Gi

Yang Pal Sang Dan Mahk Kee

Yang Soo Kwon Do Kong Kyuk

Ha Dan Kwon Soo Kong Kyuk 'Block and Strike'

Bal Ba Dahk Uro Mahk Kee

Ha Dan Mahk Kee

Bal Ba Dahk Uro Kong Kyuk
(or *Mahk Kee*, block)

Yang Pal Kong Kyuk

Son Dung Kong Kyuk

Choi Ha Dan Sweep *Jaseh*

Cap Kwon Kong Kyuk

3. One Step Sparring (*Il Soo Sik Dae Ryun*)
일수식 대련

● Number 15

The attacking member steps back with the right foot; performs a low block with the left hand and simultaneously *Ki Haps*. The senior remains in *Joon Bee Jaseh* in preparation for the rest of the exercise.

❶ The defending member *Ki Haps*, signaling to the attacker that they are ready. The attacker steps forward with the right foot and performs a middle punch with the right fist. In response the defender steps to the left with the left foot and performs an inside-outside knife hand block with the right hand in *Jun Gul Jaseh*.

❷ Using the right hand to grab the attacker's wrist, the defender uses the right leg to perform a roundhouse kick to the attacker's mid-section.

❸ Without stepping down or letting go of the attacker, the defender pulls the right foot in near the left knee and uses the right leg to perform a side kick to the attacker's knee.

❹ The defender then steps down and uses the left hand to perform a reverse upper wrist strike to the attacker's kidney. This is done while keeping a firm grip on the attacker's right wrist.

❺ The defender moves the left arm under the attacker's right arm, and in a counterclockwise motion clears the area. While clearing the area, the defender moves into front stance and uses the right fist to perform a reverse middle punch to the attacker's mid-section.

❻ Remaining in *Jun Gul Jaseh* the defender moves the right arm parallel to the body and pulls the left arm back behind the head.

❼ Immediately the defender performs a low sweeping motion with both arms, striking the back of the attacker's ankle and knee, and simultaneously *Ki Haps*. The defender's left knee is on the ground with the left arm parallel to the body and the right arm pulled back behind the head.

In closing, both members simultaneously return to *Ba Ro Jaseh* and bow. ■

• Number 16

The attacking member steps back with the left foot; performs a low block with the right hand and simultaneously *Ki Haps*. The senior remains in *Joon Bee Jaseh* in preparation for the rest of the exercise.

❶ The defending member *Ki Haps*, signaling to the attacker that they are ready. The attacker steps forward with the left foot and performs a middle punch with the left fist. In response the defender steps to the right with the right foot into *Jun Gul Jaseh* and performs an inside-outside knife hand block with the left hand.

❷ Using the left hand to grab the attacker's wrist, the defender uses the left leg to perform a roundhouse kick to the attacker's mid-section.

❸ Without stepping down or letting go of the attacker, the defender pulls the left foot in near the right knee and uses the left leg to perform a side kick to the attacker's knee.

❹The defender then steps down and uses the right hand to perform a reverse upper wrist strike to the attacker's mid-section. This is done while keeping a firm grip on the attacker's left wrist.

❺The defender moves the right arm under the attacker's left arm, and in a clockwise motion clears the area. While clearing the area, the defender moves into a front stance and uses the left fist to perform a middle punch to the attacker's mid-section.

❻Remaining in *Jun Gul Jaseh* the defender moves the left arm parallel to the body and pulls the right arm back behind the head.

❼Immediately the defender performs a low sweeping motion with both arms, striking the back of the attacker's ankle and knee, and simultaneously *Ki Haps*. The defender's right knee is on the ground with the right arm parallel to the body and the left arm pulled back behind the head.

In closing, both members simultaneously return to *Ba Ro Jaseh* and bow. ■

4. Self Defense (*Ho Sin Sool*)
호신술

• Sleeve Grab #1

Both participants begin by bowing and finding a proper distance at which to complete the exercise. The attacker proceeds by using the right hand to grab the defender's right sleeve.

❶ While keeping the elbow close to the body, the defender turns the hip completely to the left, directing the right hand downward. This first motion must be done while twisting the right hand counter clockwise to break the grip.

❷ The defender then steps forward with the left leg to the right corner at a 45⁰ while moving the right hand around in a clockwise motion holding onto the attacker's right wrist. The defender's left hand should follow to hold the attacker's elbow while it is bent. This motion should end with the defender using the right hand to hold the attacker's right wrist and the left hand to hold the attacker's right elbow straight.

❸ While maintaining the hold, the defender will perform a downward elbow strike to the attacker's right elbow or triceps. This last technique is done with a *Ki Hap*.

In closing, both members bow and return to *Ba Ro Jaseh*. ■

• Sleeve Grab #2

Both participants begin by bowing and finding a proper distance at which to complete the exercise. The attacker proceeds by using the right hand to grab the defender's right sleeve.

❶ The defender steps forward with the right leg into *Sa Ko Rip Jaseh* and moves the right arm over the attacker's right arm to break the hold.

❷ In the same stance the defender grabs hold of the attacker's right wrist, with the left hand, and performs an elbow strike with the right elbow to the attacker's head or temple. This is done while the left hand is keeping a firm grip on the attacker's wrist.

❸ Immediately the defender trades hands, using the right hand to hold onto the attacker's wrist. The defender then turns to the left into back-stance and uses the left arm to perform a spinning back elbow strike to the attacker's solar plexus. This final technique is done with a *Ki Hap*.

In closing, both members bow and return to *Ba Ro Jaseh*. ■

5. Breaking (*Kyo Pa*)
격파

● Double Break - Side Kick & Hook Kick

Both legs are used in this double breaking technique.

- ■ Break the first board with either a standing or stepping-behind side kick.
- ■ After breaking first board, immediately focus on second target.
- ■ Using opposite leg, deliver a stepping-behind hook kick.

Remember, breaking should be done as quickly as possible. Each break should take up to 1 second to perform.

6. Free Sparring Examples (*Ja Yu Dae Ryun*)
자유 대련

Down Block, Ridge Hand and Low-High Round House Kick

RED BELT
WITH 2 STRIPES

One Step Sparring
Page 212

GENERAL REQUIREMENTS
1. Sound moral character.
2. No age requirement, but must be a member of the Hwa Rang World Tang Soo Do Moo Duk Kwan Federation in good standing.
3. Regular weekly studio attendance.
4. Service to the studio.

GENERAL KNOWLEDGE
1. Conceptual knowledge of lower rank techniques.
2. Korean Tang Soo Do terminology, etiquette, and further development of Moo Duk Kwan attitudes and spirits.
3. Philosophy and history of Tang Soo Do Moo Duk Kwan.

Self Defense
Page 215

DEMONSTRATION OF ABILITY
1. **BASIC MOVEMENT (KEE CHO):**
   <u>Hand techniques</u>: All basics and combinations are required, with Hu Jin (stepping back) alone and in combination may be required.
   <u>Foot techniques</u>: Kicking combinations, hand and foot combinations moving back and forward can be required

2. **FORMS (HYUNG):**
   Pyung Ahn Oh Dan, Bassai, Chil Sung II Roh Hyung, Hwa Rang Tournament Form #3 (recommended)

Breaking
Page 217

3. **ONE STEP SPARRING (IL SOO SIK DAE RYUN):** # 15 - 18

4. **SELF DEFENSE (HO SIN SOOL):**
   Cross hand sleeve grabs # 1 - 4, all wrist grabs

5. **BREAKING (KYOK PA):** 2-point breaking: Any hand technique and jump spinning back kick

6. **FREE SPARRING (JA YU DAE RYUN)**

Free Sparring
Page 218

7. **SPECIFIC KNOWLEDGE OF CULTURE AND TERMINOLOGY:**
   Terminology of Tang Soo Do movements
   Ten Articles of Faith on Mental Training
   Ten Key Concepts
   What is the meaning of *Do*?

Control of Breathing .... 호흡 조정 *Ho Hup Cho Chung*

3. One Step Sparring (*Il Soo Sik Dae Ryun*)
일수식 대련

• Number 17

The attacking member steps back with the right foot; performs a low block with the left hand and simultaneously *Ki Haps*. The senior remains in *Joon Bee Jaseh* in preparation for the rest of the exercise.

❶The defending member *Ki Haps*, signaling to the attacker that they are ready. The attacker steps forward with the right foot and performs a middle punch with the right fist. In response the defender steps forward with the left leg and uses the left hand to perform an outside-inside palm block, while simultaneously using the right hand to perform a reverse low ridge hand attack to the attacker's groin area.

❷Immediately the attacker uses the left fist to perform a reverse middle punch. In response the defender blocks with the right hand, performing a reverse inside-out-side ridge-hand high block.

❸ The defender then steps with the left leg toward the attacker into front stance and uses the left hand to perform a middle palm strike to the attacker mid-section.

❹Immediately the defender uses the right leg to perform a jumping spinning crescent kick to the attacker's head. This kick is done with a simultaneous *Ki Hap*.

In closing, both members return to *Ba Ro Jaseh* and bow. ■

• Number 18

The attacking member steps back with the left foot; performs a low block with the right hand and simultaneously *Ki Haps*. The senior remains in *Joon Bee Jaseh* in preparation for the rest of the exercise.

❶ The defending member *Ki Haps*, signaling to the attacker that they are ready. The attacker steps forward with the left foot and performs a middle punch with the left fist. In response the defender steps forward with the right leg and uses the right hand to perform an outside-inside palm block, while simultaneously using the left hand to perform a reverse low ridge hand attack to the attacker's groin area.

❷ Immediately the attacker uses the right fist to perform a reverse middle punch. In response the defender blocks with the left hand, performing a reverse inside-outside ridge-hand high block.

❸The defender then steps with the right leg toward the attacker into front stance and uses the right hand to perform a middle palm strike to the attacker mid-section.

❹Immediately the defender uses the left leg to perform a jumping spinning crescent kick to the attacker's head. This kick is done with a simultaneous *Ki Hap*.

In closing, both members return to *Ba Ro Jaseh* and bow. ■

4. Self Defense (*Ho Sin Sool*)
호신술

• Sleeve Grab #3

Both participants begin by bowing and finding a proper distance at which to complete the exercise. The attacker proceeds by using the right hand to grab the defender's right sleeve.

❶The defender uses the left hand to strike the back of the attacker's right hand. Following this motion the defender holds the attacker's right hand close so that it is pinned against the defender's right arm. This motion is used to loosen the grip of the attacker and prepare for the next motion.

❷While keeping the elbows close to the body, the defender turns the right hand around the attacker's right hand in a clockwise motion.

❸While stepping back with the left leg into back stance, the defender applies downward pressure to the attacker's right arm. The defender must be sure to hold the attacker's hand firmly against his right arm. This to ensure that the attacker's wrist joints are locked and disable.

In closing, both members bow and return to *Ba Ro Jaseh*. ■

• Sleeve Grab #4

Both participants begin by bowing and finding a proper distance at which to complete the exercise. The attacker proceeds by using the right hand to grab the defender's right sleeve.

❶ The defender turns the right hand around the attacker's right hand in a counterclockwise fashion. While doing this, the left hand is brought underneath to grab the back of the attacker's right hand. This motion is used to loosen the grip of the attacker and prepare for the next motion.

❷ Using both hands the defender grabs the attacker's right wrist. While maintaining this hold the defender steps back with the right leg and pushes forward with both hands. This motion is used to lock-up the attacker's wrist and elbow joints, and prepare for the next motion. The attacker's fingers should be pointing upwards while the head should be facing the ground.

❸ Without letting go of the attacker, the defender uses the right leg to perform a front snap-kick to the attacker's face.

❹ Stepping down with the right leg into *Sa Ko Rip* stance, the defender performs a downward elbow strike to the back of the attacker's spine, all while maintaining control of the attacker. This last technique is done with a *Ki Hap*.

In closing, both members bow and return to *Ba Ro Jaseh*. ■

5. **Breaking** (*Kyo Pa*)
격파

- Double Break - Ridge Hand &
  Jump Spinning Back Kick

■For ridge hand strike, ensure that thumb is tucked in under hand to prevent injury.
■After breaking first board, immediately turn around, step forward, and perform a jump spinning back kick with right leg.

6. Free Sparring Examples (*Ja Yu Dae Ryun*)
자유 대련

Front arm Inside Middle Block, Back Fist, Ridge Hand
& Reverse Oblique Front Kick

CHO DAN
(MIDNIGHT BLUE)

GENERAL REQUIREMENTS

1. Sound moral character.
2. No age requirement, but must be a member of the Hwa Rang World Tang Soo Do Moo Duk Kwan Federation, in good standing.
3. Regular weekly studio attendance.
4. Service to the studio and contribution to the Hwa Rang World Tang Soo Do Moo Duk Kwan Federation.
5. Must have met minimum required evaluations by Regional Examiner or His/Her designee.

Nai Han Chi Cho Dan
Page 220

GENERAL KNOWLEDGE

1. Conceptual knowledge of lower rank techniques.
2. Assistance in teaching and class responsibilities with the ability to conduct formal classes with approval of Sa Bom - Kyo Sa.
3. Ability to explain the relationship between forms and mental discipline.

Breaking
Page 226

DEMONSTRATION OF ABILITY

1. BASIC MOVEMENT (KEE CHO):
    Hand techniques: All Korean terminology. All lower belt material may be requested.
    Foot techniques: All Korean terminology. All lower belt material may be requested.

2. FORMS (HYUNG):
    Kee Cho Hyung Sam Bu, Bassai, Chil Sung Il Roh Hyung, Nai Han Chi Cho Dan, Competition Form High Mountain Il Bu (Recommended).

Free Sparring
Page 227

3. ONE STEP SPARRING (IL SOO SIK DAE RYUN):
    # 1 - 18, 6 student creations

4. SELF DEFENSE (HO SIN SOOL): All lower belt requirements

5. BREAKING (KYOK PA):
    E Dan Yup Podo Cha Gi (Jump side kick), Reverse Punch

6. FREE SPARRING (JA YU DAE RYUN)

7. ENDURANCE (IN NEH):
    Candidate will be required to stand in *Pahl Put Ki* (Horse stance punching) minimum 120 repetitions, with proper form and power, within a 30 second time period.

8. TAKE HOME WRITTEN EXAM, WITH A 1000-WORD ESSAY ENTITLED:
"What Tang Soo Do Means to Me."

나
이
한
치

초
단

2. Nai Han Chi Cho Dan
(27 movements)

Nai Han Chi Cho Dan is a very unique form because it uses only one stance (*Kee Mah Jaseh*), also the last half of the form is an exact mirror image of the first half. Theories about the origin of the form conflict slightly. Some saying that it is the characteristic of a horse, others say it is is a form that was originally done on horse back practiced by horsemen hundreds of years ago. *Nai Han Chi Cho Dan* is not flashy but it demonstrates how to use blocking and striking techniques correctly. Good eye focus is important in this form. It is a require for obtaining a 1ˢᵗ degree black belt.

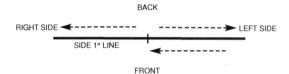

```
                    BACK
RIGHT SIDE ◀----------    ----------▶ LEFT SIDE
        SIDE 1ˢᵗ LINE    |  ◀----------
                    FRONT
```

Starting from the *Joon Bee Jaseh* position, begin inhaling while simultaneously bringing the left foot to the right knee while raising the hands in front of the face (don't blind vision). The right palm should be visible with the left hand underneath; fingers pointed toward the sky. Begin to exhale. While bending the right knee slightly, bring the left foot down to meet the right foot. Once both feet are securely planted begin to straighten the knees, while lowering the hands. Do not allow the hands to separate while they are being lowered. When finally straightening the knees and the arms, be sure to do it with a snap. The left hand should be on top with the fingers pointing toward the ground.

❶ From this position use the left foot to step in front of the right foot into *Kyo Cha Rip Jaseh.* Perform this movement with speed and snap.

❷ (*Shi Sun*: look sharply to the right). With the focus to the East (right) and the direction of the body toward the North, step to the East into *Kee Ma Jaseh* and perform a *Son Tung Kong Kyuk* (back hand) strike with the right hand.

❸ While maintaining the same stance and focus use the left elbow to perform a *Pal Koop Chi Ki* to the East.

❹ Preparation: (*Shi Sun*: Look sharply to the North and momentarily extend the arms out). Quickly pull them back so that the right arm is placed in the chamber and the left arm is carried parrallel to the body and the ground.

❺ (*Shi Sun*: look sharply to the left). Without stepping or changing the direction the body is facing, use the left arm to perform a **Ha Dan Mahk Kee** to the West.

❻ Maintaining stance and focus use the right hand to perform a half punch to the West.

A.   **B.**

❼ (*Shi Sun*: look sharply in the Northern direction). While maintaining focus use the right foot to step over the left, then step in the same direction with the left foot. Upon placing the left foot down, perfom an **Ahneso Pakuro Mahk Kee** with the right hand.

A.

B.

❽ While maintaining stance and focus, use the left fist to perform a **Ha Dan Kong Kyuk** while simultaneously performing a **Sang Dan Kong Kyuk** just behind the left side of the head with the right fist.

❾ While maintaining the same stance and focus, pull the arms apart simultaneously and use the right arm to perform a **Ha Dan Mahk Kee** to the East while using the Left fist to perform a **Cap Kwon Kong Kyuk** to the area just behind the left side of the head.

❿ While maintaining the same stance and focus, use the left arm to perform a **Pahkeso Ahnuro Mahk Kee**. The right arm should be brought up under the left for support.

Note: Moves 7 through 10 are done in quick succession.

⓫ (*Shi Sun*: look sharply to the left). While maintaining the same arm position, bring the left foot up to the side of the right knee and stomp down into *Kee Mah Jaseh* while simultaneosly performing an **Ahneso Pahkuro Mahk Kee** with the left arm to the West.

⓬ (*Shi Sun*: look sharply to the right). While maintaining the same arm position, bring the right foot up to the side of the left knee and stomp down into *Kee Mah Jaseh* while simultaneosly performing **Pakeso Ahnuro Mahk Kee** with the left arm to the East.

⓭ Preparation: (*Shi Sun*: Look sharply to the North and momentarily extend the arms out). Quickly pull them back so that the right arm is placed in the chamber and the left arm is carried parrallel to the body and the ground.

⓮ (*Shi Sun*: look sharply to the West). Use the right hand to perform a half punch to the West while simultaneously using the left fist to perform a **Wheng Jin Kong Kyuk** in the same direction. Simultaneously *Ki Hap*.

⓯ With the focus to the West (left) and the direction of the body toward the North, perform a **Son Tung Kong Kyuk** (back hand) strike with the left hand.

16 While maintaining the same stance and focus use the right elbow to perform a *Pal Koop Chi Ki* to the West.

17 Preparation: (*Shi Sun*: Look sharply to the North and momentarily extend the arms out). Quickly pull them back so that the left arm is placed in the chamber and the right arm is carried parrallel to the body and the ground.

18 (*Shi Sun*: look sharply to the right). Without stepping or changing the direction the body is facing, use the right arm to perform a *Ha Dan Mahk Kee* to the East.

19 Maintaining stance and focus use the left hand to perform a half punch to the East.

20 While maintaining focus use the left foot to step over the right, then step in the same direction with the right foot. Upon placing the right foot down. (*Shi Sun*: look sharply in the Northern direction), simultaneously perform an *Ahneso Pakuro Mahk Kee* with the left arm in the same direction.

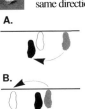

21 While maintaining stance and focus, use the right fist to perform a *Ha Dan Kong Kyuk* while simultaneously using the left fist to perform a *Sang Dan Kong Kyuk* just behind the right side of the head.

22 While maintaining the same stance and focus, pull the arms apart simultaneously, using the right arm to perform a *Ha Dan Mahk Kee* to the East while using the left fist to perform a *Cap Kwon Kong Kyuk* to the area just behind the right side of the head.

23 While maintaining the same stance and focus, use the right arm to perform a *Pahkeso Ahnuro Mahk Kee*. The left arm should be brought up under the right for support.

Note: Moves 20 through 23 are done in quick succession.

24 (*Shi Sun:* look sharply to the right). While maintaining the same arm position, bring the right foot up to the side of the left knee and stomp down into *Kee Mah Jaseh* while simultaneosly performing an *Ahneso Pahkuro Mahk Kee* with the right arm in the Western direction.

25 (*Shi Sun:* look sharply to the left). While maintaining the same arm position, bring the left foot up to the side of the right knee and stomp down into *Kee Mah Jaseh* while simultaneosly performing an *Pahkeso Ahnuro Mahk Kee* with the right arm in the Eastern direction.

26 Preparation: (*Shi Sun*: Look sharply to the North and momentarily extend the arms out). Quickly pull them back so that the left arm is placed in the chamber and the right arm is carried parrallel to the body and the ground.

27 (*Shi Sun:* look sharply to the East). Use the left fist to perform a half punch to the East while simultaneously using the left right to perform a *Wheng Jin Kong Kyuk* in the same direction. This motion is completed with the use of a *Ki Hap*.

Return to *Nai Han Chi Joon Bee.*

Applications for Nai Han Chi Cho Dan

Son Tung Kong Kyuk

Pal Koop Chi Ki

Han Dan Mahk Kee

half punch

Han Dan Mahk Kee & Cap Kwon Kong Kyuk   *Ahneso Pahkuro Mahk Kee*

Aneso Pahkuro Mahk Kee   *Wheng Jin Kong Kyuk*

5. Breaking (*Kyo Pa*)
격파

• Standing Jump Side Kick

▪Position board at chest height or above.
▪In one movement jump straight up, turn to side, and drive side kick through board(s).

6. Free Sparring Examples (*Ja Yu Dae Ryun*)
자유 대련

Inside-Outside Block, Plier Hand Strike , Knee Attack, Elbow Strike & Jump Back Kick

▶ Glossary of Terminology

Basic Terminology

Mahk Kee	Block	*Choong Shim*	Balance
Kong Kyuk	Attack	*Chung Kwon*	Forefist
Ha Dan	Low part	*Cap Kwon*	Backfist
Jung Dan	Middle part	*Soo Do*	Knife block
Sang Dan	High part	*Yuk Soo Do*	Ridge hand
Ahp	Front	*Kwan Soo*	Spear hand
Yup	Side	*Jang Kwon*	Heel of palm
Dwi	Back	*Oh Run Jok*	Right side
Cha Gi	Kick	*Wen Jok*	Left side
Ki Hap	Yell	*Tuel Oh*	Twisting
Shi Sun	Focus of eyes, Line of sight		

1. Basic Stances

Joon Be Jaseh	Ready stance	*Kee Mah Jaseh*	Horse stance
Jun Gul Jaseh	Front stance	*Sa Ko Rip Jaseh*	Side stance
Hu Gul Jaseh	Back stance	*Kyo Cha Rip Jaseh*	Cross-legged stance

2. Commands in Training

Cha Ryut	Attention	*Dwi Ro Tora*	Turn to rear
Kyung Ret	Bow	*Jin*	Movement
Joon Be	Ready	*Chun Jin*	Forward move
Si Jak	Begin	*Wheng Jin*	Sideways move
Ba Ro	Return	*Hu Jin*	Backwards move
Shio	Relax	*Yuk Jin*	Reverse movement
Tora	Turn		

3. Numbers

English	Korean	Chinese
One	*Ha Na*	*Il*
Two	*Dool*	*E*
Three	*Set*	*Sam*
Four	*Net*	*Sa*
Five	*Da Sot*	*O*
Six	*Yuh Sot*	*Yuk*
Seven	*Il Gop*	*Chil*
Eight	*Yeo Dull*	*Pahl*
Nine	*Ah Hop*	*Gu*
Ten	*Yohl*	*Sip*

4. Commands in Starting and Closing Class

Cha Ryut	Attention
Kuk Gi Bae Rae	Bow to flag
Ba Ro	Return
An Jer	Sit
Muk Nyum	Meditation
Sa Bom Nim Kae Kyung Net	Bow to Master Instructor
Kyo Sa Nim Kae Kyung Net	Bow to Certified Instructor
Sun Beh Nim Kae Kyung Net	Bow to senior member (s)
Sahng Ho Kan E Kyung Net	Bow to partner (each other)
Shim Sa Kwan Nim Ge Kyung Net	Bow to judge or examiner
Kwan Jang Nim Kae Kyung Net	Bow to the Grandmaster

5. Hands Techniques (*Soo Gi*) - Defensive

Ha Dan Mahk Kee	Low block, front stance
Sang Dan Mahk Kee	High block, front stance
Ahneso Phakuro Mahk Kee	Inside-outside block, front stance
Pahkeso Ahnuro Mahk Kee	Outside-inside block, front stance
Ssang Soo Ha Dan Mahk Kee	Two fist low block (X), front stance
Jun Gul Ssang Soo Ahneso Phakuro Mahk Kee	Two fist middle block, front stance
Ssang Soo Sang Dan Mahk Kee	Two open-hand high block, front stance
Hu Gul Ha Dan Soo Do Mahk Kee	Low knife hand block, back stance
Hu Gul Chung Dan Soo Do Mahk Kee	Middle knife hand block, back stance
Hu Gul Sang Dan Soo Do Mahk Kee	High knife hand block, back stance
Hu Gul Yup Mahk Kee	Side block, back stance
Hu Gul Ha Dan Mahk Kee	Low block, back stance
Hu Gul Sang Dan Mahk Kee	High block, back stance
Hu Gul Phakeso Ahnuro Mahk Kee	Outside-inside block, back stance

Hu Gul Sang Soo Ahneso Phakuro Mahk Kee	Two-fist middle block, back stance
Hu Gul Sang Soo Ha Dan Mahk Kee	Two-fist low block, back stance
Hu Gul Jang Kwon Phakeso Ahnero Mahk Kee	Out/In block with bottom of palm, back stance
Choi Ha Dan Soo Do Mahk Kee	Ground block with lowest knife hand
Bal Ja Ba Mahk Kee	Foothold defense, palm heels together, Cross-legged stance

6. Hand techniques (*Soo Gi*) - Offensive

Jung Dan Kong Kyuk	Middle punch, front stance
Sang Dan Kong Kyuk	High punch, front stance
Wheng Jin Kong Kyuk	Side punch, horse stance
Yuk Jin Kong Kyuk	Reverse punch, back stance
Jung Kwon	Fore fist
Cap Kwon	Back fist
Kwon Do	Hammer fist
Yuk Soo Do	Ridge hand (Reverse knife-hand)
Kwan Soo Kong Kyuk	Spear hand attack, front stance
Soo Do Kong Kyuk	Knife hand attack, front stance
Yuk Soo Do Kong Kyuk	Ridge hand attack
Hu Gul Soo Do Kong Kyuk	Knife hand attack, back stance
Jip Kye Son	Plier hand, web of thumb
Jang Kwon	Palm heel
Pal Koop Chi Kee	Elbow strike
Son Dung Kong Kyuk	Top of hand

7. Foot (Jock Gi) Attacks

Ahp Cha Nut Gi	Front snap kick
Yup Cha Nut Gi	Side kick
Hap Polder Olla Ri Gi	Front stretch kick
Yup Poder Oll Ri Gi	Side stretch kick
Yup Poder Cha Gi	Side snap kick
Aup Doll Ryo Cha Gi	Roundhouse kick
Dwi Cha Gi	Back kick
Dwi Poder Cha Gi	Back snap kick
Ahneso Phakuro Cha Gi	Inside-outside kick
Phakeso Ahnuro Cha Gi	Outside-inside kick
Dwi Ahneso Phakuro Cha Gi	Short spinning back kick
Moo Roop Cha Gi	Knee kick
Yup Hu Ri Gi	Side hook kick
Ahp Mil Er Cha Gi	Front thrust kick
Bal Ba Dak Euro Mahk Kee	Outside-inside, soul of foot block
Bal Yup Euro Mahk Kee	Outer edge of foot block

8. Colors

The colors used in the Moo Duk Kwan are the same as those used in the belt ranking system. They are:

COLOR	SEASON	MEANING
White	Winter	Emptiness, innocence, hidden potential, purity.
Green	Spring	Growth, spreading, advancement.
Red	Summer	Ripening, head (Yang), active.
Blue	Autumn	Maturity, calm (Um), passive, and harvest.

*Our traditional colors were originally just four. However, yellow and orange was officially added in 1984 under the grandmaster's approval, as an extra step for motivation between white and green belt.

9. The Uniform

The uniform or training suit is properly called Do Bok. This is a composite word combining Do "Way of life" with Bok "Apparel" or "Clothing". Since the Do Bok is what you wear while you practice your "Do" or way, its care and meaning are very important.

Similarities can be found between the current Do Bok and ancient Korean traditional clothing. Today, we maintain the white color to show purity, reverence for life, and commitment to avoid bloodshed and violence.

Action and thought are inseparable. Also the outside appearance and inside attitude are closely linked. When you look your best you usually feel good, too.

Keeping this in mind, always appear in class with your uniform clean and pressed, in good repair, and with proper trim for your rank. Your instructors or seniors will help instruct you in the proper care and wear of your Do Bok.

10. Belt and Uniform Requirements

RANK	BELT	UNIFORM
10th Gup	White	White
9th Gup	Yellow	White
8th Gup	Orange	White
7th Gup	Orange-1 blue stripe	White
6th Gup	Green	White with green lapel trim
5th Gup	Green-1 blue stripe	White with green lapel trim
4th Gup	Green-2 blue stripes	White with green lapel trim
3rd Gup	Red	White with red lapel trim
2nd Gup	Red-1 blue stripe	White with red lapel trim
1st Gup	Red-2 blue stripes	White with red lapel trim
1st Dan	Midnight blue	White with lapel, sleeves, and
2nd Dan	Midnight blue-2 white stripes	the borders trimmed
3rd Dan	Midnight blue-3 white stripes	
4th-8th Dan	Midnight blue with red stripe through middle of Belt	

Grand Master Ho Sik Pak - BODY BUILDING CHAMPION AS MR KUN SAN -1981

▶ Instructional Videos

The techniques illustrated in this book are available on video for home study. Each tape details testing requirements for one belt level, including: fundamental techniques, hand and kicking techniques, hand and foot combination, forms, self-defense, and one-step sparring.

9th GUP | **Tape 1**
Hand & foot techniques; *Kee Cho Hyung Il Bu*; One Step 1 & 2; Self Defense 1 & 2; elbow breaking technique.

8th GUP | **Tape 2**
Hand & foot techniques; *Kee Cho Hyung E Bu, Sam Bu*; One Step 3 & 4; Self-Defense 3 & 4; hammer breaking technique.

7th GUP | **Tape 3**
Hand and foot techniques; *Kee Cho Hyung Sam Bu, Pyung Ahn Cho Dan*; One Step 5 & 6; Self-Defense Straight Hand 1 & 2; stepping behind side kick breaking technique.

6th GUP | **Tape 4**
Hand and foot techniques; *Pyung Ahn Cho Dan, Ee Dan, Chil Sung E Roh Hyung*; One Step 7 & 8; Self Defense Straight Hand 3 & 4; spinning back kick breaking technique.

5th GUP | **Tape 5**
Hand and foot techniques; *Pyung Ahn Ee Dan, Sam Dan, Chil Sung Ee Roh Hyung*; One Step 9 & 10; Self-Defense Two Hand on One Hand 1 & 2; 2-point breaking techniques: reverse punch & stepping side kick.

4th GUP | **Tape 6**
Hand and foot combination; *Pyung Ahn Sam Dan, Sa Dan*; *Chil Sung E Ro Hyung*; One Step 11 & 12; Self Defense Two Hand on One Hand 3 and Two Hand on Two Hand 1 & 2; 2-point breaking techniques: knife hand and spinning back kick.

3rd GUP | **Tape 7**
Hand & foot combination; *Pyung Ahn Sa Dan, Oh Dan, Chil Sung Il Ro Hyung*; Self Defense Two Hand on Two Hand 3 & 4; One Step 13 & 14; hook kick breaking technique.

2nd GUP | **Tape 8**
Hand & foot combination; *Pyung Ahn Oh Dan, Bassai, Chil Sung Il Ro Hyung*; Self Defense Cross Hand Sleeve 1 & 2; One Step 15 & 16; Step behind side kick & hook kick breaking technique.

1st GUP | **Tape 9**
Hand and foot combination; *Pyung Ahn Oh Dan, Bassai, Chil Sung Il Roh, Nai Han Chi Cho Dan*; One Step 17 & 18; Self Defense Cross Hand Sleeves 3 & 4, choice of hand & jump spin back kick breaking techniques.

1st DAN | **Tape 10**
Hand and foot combination; *Kee Cho Hyung Sam Bu, Bassai, Chil Sung Il Roh Hyung, Nai Han Chi Cho Dan*; One Step 1-14; Self Defense; Reverse punch & standing jump side kick breaking techniques; demonstration of endurance.

2nd DAN | **Tape 11**
Hand & foot combination; *Pyung Ahn Cho Dan; Nai Han Chi Ee Dan, Jin Do, Chil Sung Sam Roh Hyung*; Self Defense against knife; *Yuk Soo Do* & jump spinning back kick breaking techniques; demonstration of endurance.

3rd DAN | **Tape 12**
Hand & foot combination; *Pyung Ahn Ee Dan, Nai Han Chi Sam Dan, Ro Hai, Chil Sung Sa Ro*; Self Defense against short stick; jump spinning heel kick breaking technique; *Da sooin Dae Ryun*; demonstration of endurance.

4th DAN | **Tape 13**
Hand & foot combination; *Pyung Ahn Sam Dan; Kong san kun, Sip soo; Chwa dae ryun* (sitting position sparring).

5th DAN | **Tape 14**
Pyung Ahn Sa Dan, Wan Shu, Sei Shan Hyung.

6th DAN | **Tape 15**
Pyung Ahn Oh Dan, Ji On Hyung, Oh Sip Sa Bo Hyung.

SELF DEFENSE | **Tape 16**
Self Defense Techniques, 9th Gup to 1st Dan.

One Step Sparing | **Tape 17**
One Step Sparring, 1-18, 9th Gup to 1st Dan.

Weapons | **Tape 18**
Weapon Techniques (*Nunchu ku*, Long stick)

Competition Forms -Gups- | **Tape 19**
Hwa Rang Competition Forms 1, 2, 3. For Gups.

Competition Forms -Dans- | **Tape 20**
High Mountain Competition Forms 1, 2, 3. For Dans.

Korean CD-Rom | **Korean Terminology CD-Rom**
Learn all the Korean terminologies by listening to Grand Master Pak. Sounds are pronounced at slow and fast speed. (available at Amazon.com)

Also inquire about our
BLACK BELT VIDEO PACKAGES and **COMPLETE TRAINING PACKAGES**

You may order by contacting:

Pak's Karate Studio
7122 Topanga Canyon Boulevard
Canoga Park, CA 91303
(818) 348-4881

▶ Index of Forms, One Step Sparring, Self Defense and Breaking

▶ Afterword

By: John Ratzenberger
May 22, 2002

Not long ago, as I drove down a sunny California street, I noticed a sign that read "Pak's Karate Tang Soo Do". As I had studied Tang Soo Do in college with Master Robert E. Beaudoin in Connecticut during the 1960's, my present need to shorten my waistline and lengthen my breath prompted me to stop and have a look. Luckily for me Grand Master Ho Sik Pak was there at the time.

Over the next few months I was delighted to find my pant size getting smaller as my kicks got higher. Master Pak was reshaping me into something that resembled a human being. Little did I know that he was also saving my life.

Because of my notoriety as an actor on the TV show CHEERS, I had been asked to lead a motorcycle charity fund raiser and arrived in Florida late one summer night. Early the next morning my host and I went and picked up my rental Harley for the next day's charity event. Twenty minutes later I was lying on the side of the highway after an 80 mph crash that separated me from the motorcycle. During my hospital stay a number of doctors who had heard about the accident visited my room out of shear curiosity. What they couldn't figure out was why I was still alive. "No body survives a crash like that", I was told repeatedly by many of the curious doctors.

The answer finally came when I happened to mention that I studied Martial Arts. Judging by my wounds it was clear then that instead of resisting the fall, I dove into it and tumbled along instead of flailing uncontrollably down the concrete. Additionally, as it was pointed out to me, the stretching involved in Master Pak's classes made me much more limber than the average 51 year old crash victim.

When I was able to return to California, Master Pak would come to my house and make me exercise even though I was coming up with some pretty good excuses why not to. In a short time I was able to go to the prescribed physical therapist who told me to her surprise that I ... "was healing like a teenager".

I am now 2nd gup and my kicks are higher still. Master Pak has not only been an excellent teacher but has become a valued friend. I know I have more lessons to learn and because of the teachings found in this book I'm still around to learn them.

Printed in Poland
by Amazon Fulfillment
Poland Sp. z o.o., Wrocław